The View from
Flyover Country

The View from Flyover Country

DISPATCHES FROM THE FORGOTTEN AMERICA

Sarah Kendzior

FLATIRON BOOKS
NEW YORK

FOR THE KIDS

www.flatironbooks.com

Library of Congress Cataloging-in-Publication Data

Names: Kendzior, Sarah, author.
Title: The view from flyover country : dispatches from the forgotten America /
    Sarah Kendzior.
Description: First edition. | New York : Flatiron Books, 2018.
Identifiers: LCCN 2017049753 | ISBN 9781250189998 (trade paperback) |
    ISBN 9781250189981 (ebook)
Subjects: LCSH: Trump, Donald, 1946– | American Dream. | United States—
    Politics and government—21st century. | United States—Social conditions—
    21st century.
Classification: LCC JK275 .K45 2018 | DDC 973.932—dc23
LC record available at https://lccn.loc.gov/2017049753

Our books may be purchased in bulk for promotional, educational, or business use.
Please contact your local bookseller or the Macmillan Corporate and Premium
Sales Department at 1-800-221-7945, extension 5442, or by email at
MacmillanSpecialMarkets@macmillan.com.

Originally published as an ebook under the same title in 2015
by Amazon Digital Services, LLC

First Flatiron Books Edition: April 2018

10 9 8 7 6 5

Contents

Introduction

The Audacity of Despair

This is a collection of essays I wrote between 2012 and 2014. It covers topics such as the collapse of the U.S. economy, the abandonment of the American heartland, the loss of opportunities for youth, the rise of paranoia and the erosion of social trust, the soaring cost of living, and the transformation of industries like media and higher education into exploitation schemes for elites. An old adage says to write what you know. As a journalist living in a decayed Midwestern city waiting—and waiting and waiting—for the Great Recession to end, that was what I knew.

Now, almost five years after I originally wrote these essays, it is still, unfortunately, what I know.

I did not set out to write a book, and I certainly did not expect this book to become a guide for those struggling to understand what happened to the United States in 2016 and the mass frustration and rifts the election of Donald Trump exposed. I simply wanted to cover what were, at the time, topics very few of my colleagues wanted to discuss: systemic corruption, the breakdown of institutions, and a post-employment economy where you pay to play or you fall through the cracks.

As the industries I worked in kept collapsing, I fell through the cracks myself a few times, and the only consolation from that experience is that the view from the cracks is a lot clearer than the view from above. I was not alone in my frustration, as I watched friends from all walks of life—people with education levels ranging from a GED to a PhD, people from all sorts of professions and backgrounds—face that same feeling of futurelessness and receive the same empty assurances. "The economy is cyclical," experts assured us, in a line that reeked of spin.

At a time when Americans were being continually informed that our crises were over—the wars in Iraq and Afghanistan were ending, we lived in a post-racial society, the good jobs would be back any day now—I saw no improvements on the ground. America had returned to "normal," politicians and pundits proclaimed, but "normal" felt like a crisis. And when you live in a crisis, you write with urgency, because you need problems to be solved.

So in the era of the audacity of hope, I made a case for the audacity of despair.

This is where you may be thinking to yourself, "Wow, this is going to be a really depressing book!" And it might be, but that never was and is not my intent. One cannot solve a problem until one acknowledges a problem exists. That is the lesson that Americans learned the hard way during the 2016 election and its aftermath.

It is easy, when people feel frightened and abandoned, for a demagogue to exploit those feelings of despair for political gain. It is easy for that demagogue to translate fear into fanaticism, to shift extremism into the mainstream and market it under the guise of populism. By the time buyer's remorse hits, a new and more brutal political culture has arisen. A gaslit nation becomes engulfed in flames.

The United States' current contentious climate is the flip side of the false promise of hope we saw half a decade ago. In the aftermath of the recession, hope was wielded like a weapon by corporations that lured in desperate Americans with exploitative assurances: work for low wages now and you will be rewarded with a raise later; rack up college debt because a steady job is guaranteed. Hope was flaunted by pundits and politicians safely ensconced in elite coastal enclaves, who implied—with their endless proclamations that prosperity awaited if you worked for it—that the lack of prospects for the rest of us must be our own fault.

Above all, we were told not to complain. Don't complain about exploitation. Don't complain about discrimination. Don't complain that you feel trapped. Don't complain, because the problem is not real—don't complain, because then people will think the problem is you.

Before I began writing about the problems of the United States, I spent my career studying authoritarian states: countries where citizens cannot complain in public because officials will punish them for doing so. Friends of mine living

in countries like Azerbaijan and Uzbekistan had been sent
to prison for talking about the same issues I wrote about in the
United States. They were criminalized for exposing institutional corruption, systemic discrimination, and opportunity-
hoarding by elites. Complaining, to me, always seemed like a
gift and an obligation, a path to prospective change that one
should never take for granted. So in the course of the two
years I spent writing these essays, I used the platform I had at
Al Jazeera to complain.

My essays went viral, often attracting millions of views
despite (or perhaps because of) their bleak subject matter.
I heard from readers living in places like St. Louis—
postindustrial regions where the economy had long bottomed
out. I heard from debt-ridden young people struggling to
survive in expensive cities where the cost of living had tri-
pled within a decade. I heard from people from all sides of
the political spectrum, who disagreed with each other on
many issues but shared a common sense of marginalization
and betrayal. I also heard from readers who were doing well,
but who felt concerned by what I reported. I tended to get
two kinds of reactions from my readers: "I'm so glad someone is finally talking about this," and "I had no idea."

In the fall of 2014, I quit Al Jazeera English following
Al Jazeera's decision to rebrand itself for an American audience, a decision which, ironically, curtailed my own ability
to talk bluntly about problems in America. (The rebranded
Al Jazeera America went out of business in early 2016.) I
moved on to covering other topics for other outlets. By that
time, my own city of St. Louis had become an international

symbol of dysfunction following protests against police brutality in Ferguson—but my old essays remained popular. My work served as a disturbing reminder that the political and economic crises I had documented not only remained, but had gotten worse. In 2015 I decided to collect the essays I had written for Al Jazeera, to call the collection *The View from Flyover Country*, and to sell it on the Internet.

After the 2016 election, *The View from Flyover Country* became an online bestseller. This was partially due to the fact that I had predicted nearly all developments of the 2016 election and Trump's win—my foresight was an unfortunate by-product of a lifetime spent studying foreign demagogues, along with an intimate understanding of deteriorating conditions in the United States. But my book also became popular because the issues I had started writing about way back in 2012 never lost relevance. They had simmered and then exploded, startling elites who still thought of our country as one of prosperity and possibility. Because I had tracked the death of the American dream in real time, and because I focused on those who suffered, many people turned to my book for an explanation.

Today, the problems I exposed in *The View from Flyover Country*, which were controversial five years ago, are now a part of mainstream political discourse. This would be a matter of profound relief if I believed the result was that they would be remedied instead of exploited.

As the book gained popularity, I stayed where I am: in an impoverished blue city in a bright-red state, squarely in the center of the country. In the publishing world, this makes me an anomaly. In the 2015 introduction to this book, I wrote, "This is the view from the other America, from flyover country, the places and people often ignored." Two years later, we are still ignored. The Midwest, in decline for decades, still suffers disproportionately. We get attention when there's a murder, a protest, an election. Otherwise, we are treated as pawns in a media-staged hunger games, as parachute journalists swoop in for riots and rallies, as people who would never deign to live in a place like my city tell the world what it truly represents, who we truly are.

As a result, the complexity of our plight—and of America's in general—has often been misconstrued. Since the 2000 elections, pundits have been proclaiming there are "two Americas," red and blue. This has never truly been the case. There are dozens of red Americas, with extreme variations in demographics and values, and dozens of blue Americas as well. There are endless variations of "America" in St. Louis alone. There is no America that is "real" or "fake." This insistence that we have an inherent divide has in some respects become a self-fulfilling prophecy. At this contentious point in our history, these divergent Americas are unified most, unfortunately, by a collective sense of pain. America is purple—purple like a bruise.

I live in the middle, and when you live in the middle, you see things from all sides.

This edition of *The View from Flyover Country* contains the original essays in their original form because my goal has not changed. I am motivated today by the same thing that motivated me when I first wrote these pieces: I believe that problems, if exposed and documented, can be solved, and that suffering can be abated. It's never clear what the result of discussing problems will be, but ignoring them is a clear road to destruction.

Blind hope, in the end, is only blindness. If we want to figure out a way out of this situation, we need to reexamine how we got into it.

—September 2017

PART I

Flyover Country

The View from
Flyover Country

n St. Louis, you can buy a mansion for $275,000. It has
twelve bedrooms, eight bathrooms, a three-bedroom carriage house, and is surrounded by vacant lots. It was built
in the late 1800s, a few decades before the 1904 World's
Fair, when St. Louis was the pride of America. In 1904,
everyone wanted to live in St. Louis. A century later, the
people who live here die faster. A child born in Egypt, Iran,
or Iraq will live longer than a child born in north St. Louis.
Almost all the children born in north St. Louis are black.

In St. Louis, the museums are free. At the turn of the
twentieth century, the city built a pavilion. They drained the
wetlands and made a lake and planted thousands of trees and
created a park. They built fountains at the base of a hillside
and surrounded it with promenades, white and gleaming.
Atop the hill is an art museum with an inscription cut in
stone: "Dedicated to art and free to all." On Sundays, children

do art projects in a gallery of Max Beckmann paintings. Admission is free, materials are free, because in St. Louis art is for everyone.

In St. Louis, you can walk twenty minutes from the mansions to the projects. In one neighborhood, the kids from the mansions and the kids from public housing go to the same public school. On the walls of the school cafeteria are portraits of Martin Luther King Jr. and Barack Obama, to remind the children what leaders look like.

In St. Louis, the murder rate is high and the mayor is named Slay but few think that is funny. In St. Louis, things are cheap but life stays hard. In St. Louis, an African-American man with gold teeth and a hoodie and baggy jeans rushed toward me in a mall, because I was pushing a baby carriage, and he wanted to hold the door open for me.

Ahead of Its Time

St. Louis is one of those cities that does not make it into the international news unless something awful happens, like it did last week in Cleveland, another American heartland city with a bad reputation and too many black people to meet the media comfort zone. The city is treated like a joke, and the people who live there and rescue women and make concise indictments of American race relations are turned into memes.

St. Louis is one of those cities where, if you are not from there, people ask why you live there. You tell them how it is a secret wonderland for children; how the zoo is free and

the parks are beautiful; how people are more kind and gen-
erous than you would imagine; how it is not as dangerous as
everyone says. They look at you skeptically and you know
that they are thinking you cannot afford to move. They are
right, but that is only part of it.

St. Louis is one of those cities that is always ahead
of its time. In 1875, it was called the "Future Great City of
the World." In the nineteenth
century, it lured in traders and
explorers and companies that
funded the city's public works
and continue to do so today. In
the twentieth century, St. Louis
showed the world ice cream and
hamburgers and ragtime and
blues and racism and sprawl
and riots and poverty and sudden, devastating decay. In the
twenty-first century, St. Louis is starting to look more like
other American cities, because in the twenty-first century,
America has started looking more like St. Louis.

> This is the view from
> flyover country, where
> the rich are less rich
> and the poor are more
> poor and everyone has
> fewer things to lose.

St. Louis is a city where people are doing so much with
so little that you start to wonder what they could do if they
had more.

Rich Are Less Rich

In St. Louis, you reevaluate "fair." In St. Louis, you
might have it bad, but someone's got it worse. This is the
view from flyover country, where the rich are less rich and

the poor are more poor, and everyone has fewer things
to lose.

The symbol of St. Louis is both a gateway and a memorial. The Arch mirrors the sky and shadows the city. It is
part of a complex that includes the courthouse where the
Dred Scott case was settled, ruling that African Americans
were not citizens and that slavery had no bounds.

On a St. Louis street corner, someone is wearing a sign
that says, "I Am a Man." Like most in the crowd gathered
outside a record store parking lot, he is African-American.
He is a fast food worker and he is a protester. He needs to
remind you he is a human being because it has been a long
time since he was treated like one.

On May 8, 2013, dozens of fast food workers in St. Louis
went on strike in pursuit of fairer wages and benefits. "We
can't survive on 735!" they cried, referring to their wage of
$7.35 an hour—a wage so low you can work forty hours a
week and still fall below the poverty line. At a rally on
May 9, workers from Hardee's and Church's Chicken talked
about what they would do with $15 an hour: feed their fam-
ilies, pay their bills. "If we can make a living wage, we can
give back to the community, and we are part of this community," a cashier from Chipotle said.

In St. Louis, possibilities are supposed to be in the past.
It is the closest thing America has to a fallen imperial capital. This is where dystopian Hollywood fantasies are set and
filmed. It is the gateway and the memorial of the American
Dream.

But when the American Dream is dying for everyone,

St. Louis might be the one to rise up. In St. Louis, people know what happens when social mobility stalls, when lines harden around race and class. They know that if you have a job and work hard, you should be able to do more than survive. They know that every person, every profession, is worthy of dignity and respect.

St. Louis is no longer a city where you come to be somebody. But you might leave it a better person.

—Originally published May 12, 2013

Expensive Cities Are Killing Creativity

On May 5, musician Patti Smith was asked what advice she had for young people trying to make it in New York City. The longtime New Yorker's take? Get out. "New York has closed itself off to the young and the struggling," she said. "New York City has been taken away from you."

Smith was not the only New Yorker to reject the city that had nurtured artists for decades. In October, musician David Byrne argued that "the cultural part of the city—the mind—has been usurped by the top 1 percent." Under Michael Bloomberg, New York's first billionaire mayor, homelessness and rent both soared, making one of the world's centers of creative and intellectual life unlivable for all but its richest citizens.

At play, notes Byrne, was more than a rise in the cost of living. It was a shift in the perceived value of creativity, backed by an assumption that it must derive from and be tied to wealth. "A culture of arrogance, hubris and winner-take-all was established," he recalls. "It wasn't cool to be poor or struggling. The bully was celebrated and cheered."

New York—and San Francisco, London, Paris, and other cities where the cost of living has skyrocketed—are no longer places where you go to be someone. They are places you live when you are born having arrived. They are, as journalist Simon Kuper puts it, "the vast gated communities where the one percent reproduces itself."

There are exceptions in these cities, but they tend to survive by serving the rule. *The New York Times* recently profiled Sitters Studio, a company that sends artists and musicians into the homes of New York's wealthiest families to babysit their children. "The artist-as-babysitter can be seen as a form of patronage," suggests the *Times*, "in which lawyers, doctors and financiers become latter-day Medicis."

This is the New York artist today: a literal servant to corporate elites, hired to impart "creativity" to children whose bank accounts outstrip their own.

The *Times* explains the need for the company as follows: "Parents keep hearing that, in the cutthroat future, only the creative will survive." The "creative" will survive—but what of creativity? Enterprises like Sitters Studio posit creativity as commodification: a taught skill that bolsters business prowess for tiny corporate heirs.

Creativity—as an expression of originality, experimentation, innovation—is not a viable product. It has been priced out into irrelevance—both by the professionalization of the industries that claim it, and the soaring cost of entry to those professions.

The "creative class" is a frozen archetype—one that does not boost the economy of global cities, as urban studies theorist Richard Florida argues, but is a product of their takeover by elites. The creative class plays by the rules of the rich, because those are the only rules left. Adaptation is a form of survival. But adaptation is a form of abandonment as well.

Bias Against Creativity

In an article for *Slate*, Jessica Olien debunks the myth that originality and inventiveness are valued in U.S. society: "This is the thing about creativity that is rarely acknowledged: Most people don't actually like it."

She cites academic studies indicating that people are biased against creative minds. They crave the success of the result, but shun the process that produces it: the experimentation that may yield to failure, the rejection of social norms that breeds rejection of the artist herself.

Today, creative industries are structured to minimize the diversity of their participants—economically, racially, and ideologically. Credentialism, not creativity, is the passport to entry.

Over the past decade, as digital media made it possible for anyone, anywhere, to share their ideas and work, barriers to professional entry tightened and geographical proximity became valued. Fields where advanced degrees were once a rarity—art, creative writing—now view them as a requirement. Unpaid internships and unpaid labor are rampant, blocking off industry access for those who cannot work without pay in the world's most expensive cities.

Yet to discuss it, as artist Molly Crabapple notes in her brilliant essay "Filthy Lucre," is verboten. Recalling her years as a struggling artist, she remembers being told by a fellow artist—a successful man living off his inherited money—that a "real artist" must live in poverty.

> As digital media made it possible for anyone, anywhere, to share their ideas and work, barriers to professional entry tightened and geographical proximity became valued.

"What the artist was pretending he didn't know is that money is the passport to success," she writes. "We may be free beings, but we are constrained by an economic system rigged against us. What ladders we have are being yanked away. Some of us will succeed. The possibility of success is used to call the majority of people failures."

Failure, in an economy of extreme inequalities, is a source of fear. To fail in an expensive city is not to fall but to plummet. In expensive cities, the career ladder comes with a drop-off to hell, where the fiscal punishment for risk gone wrong is more than the average person can endure. As a result, innovation is stifled, conformity encouraged. The creative class becomes the leisure class—or they work to serve the latter's needs, or they abandon their fields entirely.

Nothing to Fear . . .

But creative people should not fear failure. Creative people should fear the prescribed path to success—its narrowness, its specificity, its reliance on wealth and elite approval. When success is a stranglehold, true freedom is failure. The freedom to fail is the freedom to innovate, to experiment, to challenge.

In 2012, St. Louis artist Martin Brief debuted his drawing "Success." The drawing consisted only of a dictionary definition of success, with each word broken down into its own definition, until, as he writes, "the language can be read but will not yield any greater understanding of what the word means."

It is a mockery of careerism made all the more salient by Brief's residence in St. Louis—where success, by definition, is supposed to be impossible. To "succeed," one is supposed to leave a city like St. Louis—a Middle-American city associated with poverty and crime. To "succeed" is to embody the definition of contemporary success: sanctioned, sanitized, solvent.

But sanctioned success is dependent on survival, and it is hard for most people to survive in an art world capital like New York, where some homeless people work two jobs. Success by geographical proxy comes with a price: purchased freedom for the rich, serving the rich for the rest. But what happens when we veer off that path? Is it failure? Or is it redefined, recognized anew?

Creativity is sometimes described as thinking outside the box. Today the box is a gilded cage. In a climate of careerist conformity, cheap cities with bad reputations—where, as art critic James McAnally notes, "no one knows whether it is possible for one to pursue a career"—may have their own advantage. "In the absence of hype, ideas gather, connections build, jagged at first, inarticulate," McAnally writes of St. Louis. "Then, all of a sudden, worlds emerge."

Perhaps it is time to reject the "gated citadels"—the cities powered by the exploitation of ambition, the cities where so much rides on so little opportunity. Reject their prescribed and purchased paths, as Smith implored, for cheaper and more fertile terrain. Reject the places where you cannot speak out, and create, and think, and fail. Open your eyes to where you are, and see where you can go.

—Originally published December 17, 2013

The Peril of Hipster Economics

O n May 16, an artist, a railway service and a government agency spent $291,978 to block poverty from the public eye.

Called "psychylustro," German artist Katharina Grosse's project is a large-scale work designed to distract Amtrak train riders from the dilapidated buildings and fallen factories of north Philadelphia. The city has a 28 percent poverty rate—the highest of any major U.S. city—with much of it concentrated in the north. In some north Philadelphia elementary schools, nearly every child is living below the poverty line.

Grosse partnered with the National Endowment of the Arts and Amtrak to mask north Philadelphia's hardship with a delightful view. A *Wall Street Journal* headline calls this "Fighting Urban Blight With Art." Liz Thomas, the curator of the project, calls it "an experience that asks people to think about this space that they hurtle through every day."

The project is not actually fighting blight, of course—only the ability of Amtrak customers to see it.

"I need the brilliance of color to get close to people, to stir up a sense of life experience and heighten their sense of presence," Grosse proclaims.

"People," in Grosse and Thomas's formulation, are not those who actually live in north Philadelphia and bear the brunt of its burdens. "People" are those who can afford to view poverty through the lens of aesthetics as they pass it by.

Urban decay becomes a set piece to be remodeled or romanticized. This is hipster economics.

Influx of Hipsters

In February, director Spike Lee delivered an impassioned critique—derisively characterized as a "rant" by U.S. media outlets—on the gentrification of New York City. Arguing that an influx of ". . . hipsters" had driven up rent in most neighborhoods—and in turn driven out the African-American communities that once called them home—he noted how long-dormant city services suddenly reappeared:

"Why does it take an influx of white New Yorkers in the south Bronx, in Harlem, in Bed Stuy, in Crown Heights for the facilities to get better? The garbage wasn't picked up every . . . day when I was living in 165 Washington Park . . . So, why did it take this great influx of white people to get the schools better? Why's there more police protection in Bed Stuy and Harlem now? Why's the garbage getting picked up more regularly? We been here!"

Lee was criticized by many for "hipster-bashing," including African-American professor John McWhorter, who claimed that "hipster" was a "sneaky way of saying 'honkey'" and compared Lee to television character George Jefferson.

These dismissals, which focus on gentrification as culture, ignore that Lee's was a critique of the racist allocation of resources. Black communities whose complaints about poor schools and city services go unheeded find these complaints are readily addressed when wealthier, whiter people move in. Meanwhile, longtime locals are treated as contagions on the landscape, targeted by police for annoying the new arrivals.

Gentrifiers focus on aesthetics, not people. Because people, to them, are aesthetics.

Proponents of gentrification will vouch for its benevolence by noting it "cleaned up the neighborhood." This is often code for a literal whitewashing. The problems that existed in the neighborhood—poverty, lack of opportunity, struggling populations denied city services—did not go away. They were simply priced out to a new location.

That new location is often an impoverished suburb, which lacks the glamour to make it the object of future renewal efforts. There is no history to attract preservationists because there is nothing in poor suburbs viewed as worth preserving, including the futures of the people forced to live in them. This is blight without beauty, ruin without romance: payday loan stores, dollar stores, unassuming homes, and unpaid bills. In the suburbs, poverty looks banal and is overlooked.

In cities, gentrifiers have the political clout—and accompanying racial privilege—to reallocate resources and repair infrastructure. The neighborhood is "cleaned up" through the removal of its residents. Gentrifiers can then bask in "urban life"—the storied history, the selective nostalgia, the carefully sprinkled grit—while avoiding responsibility to those they displaced.

Hipsters want rubble with guarantee of renewal. They want to move into a memory they have already made.

Impoverished Suburbs

In a sweeping analysis of displacement in San Francisco and its increasingly impoverished suburbs, journalist Adam Hudson notes that "gentrification is trickle-down economics applied to urban development: the idea being that as long as a neighborhood is made suitable for rich and predominantly white people, the benefits will trickle down to everyone else." Like trickle-down economics itself, this theory does not play out in practice.

Rich cities such as New York and San Francisco have become what journalist Simon Kuper calls gated citadels, "vast gated communities where the one percent reproduces itself."

Struggling U.S. cities of the Rust Belt and heartland lack the investment of coastal contemporaries, but have in

turn been spared the rapid displacement of hipster economics. Buffered by their eternal uncoolness, these slow-changing
cities have a chance to make better choices—choices that
value the lives of people over the aesthetics of place.

In an April blog post, Umar Lee, a St. Louis writer and
full-time taxi driver, bemoaned the economic model of
ride-share services, which are trying to establish themselves
in the city. Noting that they hurt not only taxi drivers but
poor residents who have neither cars nor public transport and
thus depend on taxis willing to serve dangerous neighborhoods, he dismisses Uber and Lyft as hipster elitists
masquerading as innovators:

"I've heard several young hipsters tell me they're socially-
liberal and economic-conservative, a popular trend in
American politics," he writes. "Well, I hate to break it to
you, buddy, but it's economics and the role of the state that
defines politics. If you're an economic conservative, despite
how ironic and sarcastic you may be or how tight your jeans
are, you, my friend, are a conservative . . ."

Lee tells me he has his own plan to try to mitigate the
negative effects of gentrification, which he calls "50-50-20-
15." All employers who launch businesses in gentrifying
neighborhoods should have a workforce that is at least 50
percent minorities, 50 percent people from the local neighborhood, and 20 percent ex-offenders. The employees
should be paid at least $15 per hour.

Gentrification spreads the myth of native incompetence:
that people need to be imported to be important, that a sign
of a neighborhood's "success" is the removal of its poorest

residents. True success lies in giving those residents the services and opportunities they have long been denied.

When neighborhoods experience business development, priority in hiring should go to locals who have long struggled to find nearby jobs that pay a decent wage. Let us learn from the mistakes of New York and San Francisco, and build cities that reflect more than surface values.

—Originally published May 29, 2014

Mourn the Fall of the Mall

n 1978, George Romero debuted *Dawn of the Dead,* a movie about flesh-eating zombies who converge on a U.S. shopping mall. Released when malls had begun to supplant downtowns as centers of commerce, *Dawn of the Dead* critiqued the conformity and consumerism of 1970s America.

"It's some kind of instinct," one character explains, as brain-dead zombies stumble past escalators and chain stores. "Memory of what they used to do. This was an important place in their lives."

In 2012, Gillian Flynn released *Gone Girl,* a thriller that—in its portrayal of economic desperation, desolation, and deception—is arguably the great novel of the recession. Like *Dawn of the Dead, Gone Girl* stages a key scene in a mall, only here the mall itself is the horror. Returning to his Midwest hometown, *Gone Girl*'s narrator visits his old shopping grounds only to find a graveyard of U.S. enterprise, a shattered structure of shuttered stores where the unemployed seek shelter and drugs.

"I'd expected the mall smell as we entered: the temperature-controlled hollowness," the narrator observes. "Instead, I smelled old grass and dirt . . . It was suburbia, post-comet, post-zombie, post-humanity."

Malls no longer breed zombie shoppers. Instead, they are graveyards of the U.S. economy. Gone are the brain-dead consumers of a more decadent past, when there were things to buy and buyers to sell them and places with people inside.

Now we are zombies with nothing to eat.

Since 2008, hundreds of malls across the U.S. have shut down, and half of all U.S. malls are predicted to close within the next ten years. Thwarted shoppers visit online mall mortuaries like DeadMalls and Labelscar, where they post photos of their decimated economic landscapes. Others strip the malls for parts, stealing scrap material found inside.

Who would have guessed, a decade ago, that the most valuable part of the mall's brick-and-mortar economy would be the brick and mortar?

Mall Memories

Some rejoice at the fall of the mall, hopeful that it will lead to the revitalization of downtown commercial districts.

This is a faulty assumption. Cities doing well enough to rebuild their downtowns likely did not depend on the mall in the first place.

The mall has long been derided by those with the luxury of an alternative. When the U.S. industrial economy faltered in the 1970s, downtowns in many cities crumbled, and shopping malls—homogeneous, enclosed, and sterile— both enabled and compensated for their demise.

In the media, malls were pilloried as monoliths devoid of character. Mockery of the mall spurred pop culture prototypes: vacuous Valley girls, meandering mall rats. Underlying the mockery was grief for the loss of a seemingly more connected and welcoming urban life: the independent businesses, local markets, and community ties built around them.

Advice by algorithm, delivery by drone: this is what a dehumanized landscape looks like.

But while these were memories for some, for others they were merely rumors. A functional local economy was a story our parents told us.

For U.S. citizens raised in cities of post-industrial blight, there was the mall and the mall alone. We did not "choose" between supporting the mall or the local businesses, because by the time we came of age there were few local businesses left to support. There were no independent boutiques and bookstores to protect from corporate takeover: such battles were plot devices of movies set in more cultured places. We watched from afar, wondering what it was like to have something to lose. Our rundown towns had little anyone wanted: empty lots, boarded windows, vacant stores.

Decades passed, and no one rebuilt them. Now the malls follow, and no one will rebuild them either.

My generation watches the malls fall like our parents watched the downtowns die. To our children, the mall will be a nostalgic abstraction, a 404 in concrete.

Online Substitute?

The rise in online shopping has been blamed for the demise of the mall. But some economic analysts see a more basic problem.

"What's going on is the customers don't have the [. . .] money," notes longtime retail consultant Howard Davidow-itz. "That's it. This isn't rocket science."

Between 2000 and 2011, suburban poverty surged 67 percent, as gentrification forced city residents from their homes. Mid-tier malls that depended on middle-class shoppers faltered, as the middle class shrank.

"They're marginal malls because they're in marginal areas, in many cases," says retail analyst Kenneth Dalto, noting how demographic shifts have drained the revenue base.

The fall of the mall is a problem for the consumer: with local businesses decimated and chain stores departed, those without Internet access and credit cards can struggle to procure goods. But the fall of the mall is a bigger problem for low-skill workers.

Materialism may remain rampant, but now its spaces are secret. Retail work has been replaced with jobs in online shopping warehouses where "pickers" labor unseen in brutal conditions.

"We are machines, we are robots, we plug our scanner in, we're holding it, but we might as well be plugging it into ourselves. We don't think for ourselves, maybe they don't trust us to think for ourselves as human beings, I don't know," says Adam Littler, who worked undercover at an Amazon warehouse to witness conditions firsthand. On a given night shift he walked ten miles and was expected to collect an order every thirty-three seconds.

Malls were once castigated for turning consumers into zombies. Now, the zombie is the ideal online retail employee, unthinking and robotic. Advice by algorithm, delivery by drone: this is what a dehumanized landscape looks like.

Our connections and commerce are dependent on our screens. Pay attention, pay attention, to the men behind the screens.

"When there's no more room in hell, the dead will walk the earth," the *Dawn of the Dead* trailer intoned thirty-five years ago. There is plenty of room in this hell: downtowns replaced by malls replaced by nothing. Old deserted buildings in cities, new deserted buildings in suburbs, always an available parking space, always a worker desperate for work.

Do not rejoice at the fall of the mall. The setting may have been artificial, but the people in it were real.

—Originally published July 1, 2014

PART II

The Post-Employment
Economy

Surviving the Post-Employment Economy

A lawyer. A computer scientist. A military analyst. A teacher.

What do these people have in common? They are trained professionals who cannot find full-time jobs. Since 2008, they have been tenuously employed—working one-year contracts, consulting on the side, hustling to survive. They spent thousands on undergraduate and graduate training to avoid that hustle. They eschewed dreams—journalism, art, entertainment—for safer bets, only to discover that the safest bet is that your job will be contingent and disposable.

Unemployed graduates are told that their predicament is their own fault. They should have chosen a more "practical" major, like science or engineering, and stayed away from the fickle and loathsome humanities. The reality is that, in the "jobless recovery," nearly every sector of the economy has been decimated. Companies have turned permanent jobs into contingency labor, and entry-level positions into unpaid internships.

Changing your major will not change a broken economy.

People Devalued

In the United States, 9 percent of computer science graduates are unemployed, and 14.7 percent of those who hold degrees in information systems have no job. Graduates with degrees in STEM—science, technology, engineering, and medicine—are facing record joblessness, with unemployment at more than twice pre-recession levels. The job market for law degree holders continues to erode, with only 55 percent of 2011 law graduates in full-time jobs. Even in the military, that behemoth of the national budget, positions are being eliminated or becoming contingent due to the sequestration.

It is not skills or majors that are being devalued. It is people.

Academics face particular derision for their choice of profession. "You got a PhD—what did you expect?" they are told when they note that 76 percent of professors work without job security, usually for poverty wages.

It is true that the academic job market has been terrible for decades. But until 2008, PhD's could have expected more. Since 2009, most academic disciplines have lost roughly 40 percent of their positions, while the backlog of qualified candidates continues to grow. Most PhD's work as adjunct faculty or in the new, euphemistic sectors of high-brow im-poverishment: "non-stipendiary fellow," "special assistant professor," or "voluntary development opportunity."

Best of Bad Options

Despite the dire employment conditions of higher edu-cation, young people continue to enroll in graduate school. Detractors roll their eyes: Why would a young person spend years earning a degree of questionable value? Why not "go get a job"? To which the twenty-something laughs, having graduated into an economy where peers spend years vainly looking for a job, finding only unpaid internships or low-wage contingency labor, often while living at home. A funded graduate program, with health insurance, seems a welcome escape.

"But it is not just about your current earnings," the de-tractor continues. "It is about the wages you lose while in the program." To which the thirty-something, having spent her adult life in an economy of stagnant wages and eroding opportunities, takes the twenty-something aside and explains that this is a maxim she and her peers, too, were told, but from which they never benefitted. She tells the twenty-something what she already knows: it is hard to plan for what is already gone.

We live in the tunnel at the end of the light.

If you are thirty-five or younger—and quite often, older—the advice of the old economy does not apply to you. You live in the post-employment economy, where corporations have decided not to pay people. Profits are still high. The money is still there. But not for you. You will work without a pay raise, benefits, or job security. Survival is now a laudable aspiration.

Higher education is merely a symptom of a broader economic disease. As universities boast record endowments and spend millions on lavish infrastructure, administrators justify poor treatment of faculty, or "lecturers," by noting that they: 1) "choose" to work for poverty wages, and 2) picked specializations that give them limited "market value"—ignoring, of course, that almost no one is valued in this market, save those who are reaping its greatest profits.

The college-major debate—in which "skill" is increasingly redefined as a specific corporate contribution—extends this inequity to the undergraduate level, defining as worthless both the student's field of study and the person teaching it. But when worthlessness is determined by the people handing out—or withholding—monetary worth, we have cause for reassessment.

Failure of the System

It is easy to decry a broken system. It is harder to figure out how to live in it.

What must be made clear is that this is not a crisis of individual choices. It is a systemic failure—within higher education and beyond. It is a crisis of managed expectations—expectations of what kind of job is "normal," what kind of treatment is to be tolerated, and what level of sacrifice is reasonable.

When survival is touted as an aspiration, sacrifice becomes a virtue. But a hero is not a person who suffers. A suffering person is a person who suffers.

If you suffer in the proper way—silently, or with proclaimed fealty to institutions—then you are a hard worker "paying your dues." If you suffer in a way that shows your pain, that breaks your silence, then you are a complainer—and you are said to deserve your fate.

But no worker deserves to suffer. To compound the suffering of material deprivation with rationalizations for its warrant is not only cruel to the individual but gives exploiters moral license to prey.

Individuals internalize the economy's failure as a media chorus excoriates them over what they should have done differently. They jump to meet shifting goalposts; they express gratitude for their own mistreatment: their unpaid labor, their debt-backed devotion, their investment in a future that never arrives.

And when it does not arrive, and they wonder why, they are told they were stupid to expect it. They stop talking, because humiliation is not a bargaining chip. Humiliation is a price you pay in silence—and with silence.

People can always make choices. But the choices of today's workers are increasingly limited. Survival is not only a matter of money, it is a matter of mentality—of not mistaking bad luck for bad character, of not mistaking lost opportunities for opportunities that were never really there.

You are not your job. But you are how you treat people.

So what can you do? You can work your hardest and do

your best. You can organize and push for collective change. You can hustle and scrounge and play the odds.

But when you fall, know that millions are falling with you. Know that it is, to a large extent, out of your hands. And when you see someone else falling, reach out your hands to catch them.

—*Originally published November 3, 2013*

Meritocracy for Sale

O n April 24, 2013, the Robert F. Kennedy Center for Justice and Human Rights announced it was having an auction to raise money to "carry forward Robert Kennedy's dream of a more just and peaceful world." Through the auction website Charitybuzz, bidders could compete for a variety of prizes: a visit to the set of *Teenage Mutant Ninja Turtles*, a personal meeting with Ryan Seacrest, a tour of Jay Leno's car collection. Or a six-week unpaid internship at the United Nations, where the recipient will "gain inside knowledge of just how the UN really operates." The listed current bid? Twenty-two thousand dollars.

"This truly is the ultimate internship opportunity for any college or graduate student looking to get their foot in the door," the website proclaimed. For more than what many colleges cost in annual tuition, the highest bidder would receive "tremendous opportunities to make invaluable connections."

One would suspect that a college student who can pay $22,000 to work twenty-five hours a week for free in one of the most expensive cities in the world needs little help making connections. But that misconstrues the goal of unpaid internships: transforming personal wealth into professional credentials. For students seeking jobs at certain policy organizations, the way to get one's foot in the door is to walk the streets paved in gold. In the post-employment economy, jobs are privileges, and the privileged have jobs.

Unpaid and "pay to play" internships have long dominated policy fields, but the $22,000 asking price signified a barrier to entry so galling the UN issued a statement in response. "Internships at the United Nations are not for sale and cannot be put up for auction. We are trying to find out the details of how this came about and have contacted charitybuzz.com," a UN representative wrote to Inner City Press, who reported on the case.

When the story broke, I contacted Charitybuzz, who confirmed the auction's existence and said they would speak to their "contact at the UN" for details. The Robert F. Kennedy Center continues to list the auction under the tagline "Spend six weeks as a United Nations intern with Bruce Knotts and the UN Committee on Human Rights," while the UN continues to deny it without offering details. It is difficult to tell what is going on. Whatever the end game, someone is willing to drop $22,000 to play it.

Barriers to Entry

UN internships may not be up for auction, but they are, in essence, for sale. The United Nations does not pay its interns, making it very difficult for someone who is not independently wealthy to take an internship. The only thing that distinguishes the alleged auction from the UN's normal practice is that the unspoken class discrimination is made blatant.

"Given the high cost of living in key UN cities, such as New York and Geneva, undertaking a UN internship is an experience that few can afford, especially those from the very developing countries the organization strives to serve," wrote the group Unpaid Is Unfair in a 2012 petition calling on the United Nations to stop using free labor.

Their call went unheeded. The United Nations' website includes a form for calculating the personal expenses an intern incurs—expenses the UN conservatively estimates at $2,500 per month, not counting travel to New York City or health insurance. Interns are forbidden from taking other paid work during their two-month term, and they are not allowed to apply for jobs at the UN for six months following the internship. "A possible source of employment would be the United Nations Volunteers Program," the UN website suggests. This program pays no salary.

"For an organization that prides itself on inclusion, diversity, and equality, the UN's refusal to compensate its interns has created a system that counters those very ideals," writes former UN intern Matt Hamilton, noting that only

5 percent of UN interns come from the least developed
countries. Young people who care about international justice—
including those who witness firsthand its erosion in poor,
repressive states—cannot afford to work jobs structured on
noblesse oblige.

The United Nations is far from the only organization refusing to pay its interns. Most human rights, policy, and
development organizations pay interns nothing, but will not
hire someone for a job if he or she lacks the kind of experience an internship provides. Privilege is recast as perseverance. The end result hurts individuals struggling in the
labor market but also restructures the market itself.

Unpaid internships lock out millions of talented young
people based on class alone. They send the message that
work is not labor to be compensated with a living wage, but
an act of charity to the powerful, who reward the unpaid
worker with "exposure" and "experience." The promotion of
unpaid labor has already eroded opportunity—and quality—
in fields like journalism and politics. A false meritocracy
breeds mediocrity.

Worst of all, unpaid internships in policy and human
rights send the message that fighting poverty, inequality, and
other issues of injustice is something that only rich people
should do. Qualities that should be encouraged in society—
like empathy and the willingness to stand up for others—are
devalued when ordinary people are told that they literally
cannot afford to care.

"I think right-wing populists hate the 'liberal elite' more
than economic elites because they've grabbed all the jobs

where you get paid to do something that isn't just for the money—the pursuit of art, or truth, or charity," notes David Graeber, an anthropologist whose ideas helped shape the Occupy movement. "All they can do if they want to do something bigger than themselves and still get paid is join the army."

Fair and Just

On the day the story of the alleged $22,000 UN internship broke, *New York Times* columnist Thomas Friedman assured us that our world is fair and just. After proclaiming that the world is "tailored for the self-motivated" and the "boundaries are all gone," he argued, "We're entering a world that increasingly rewards individual aspiration and persistence and can measure precisely who is contributing and who is not. This is not going away, so we better think how we help every citizen benefit from it."

While perhaps an argument unto itself on the erosion of meritocracy—some were fooled into thinking it was created by the parody website Thomas Friedman Op/Ed Generator—Friedman's column sheds light on how the wealthy tend to believe our economy works.

Friedman encourages young people to "invest in themselves," seemingly unaware of how literal an investment this is nowadays, and how few young people have the resources to do so. He praises hard work, but he does not acknowledge the dreams deferred—the young people who would give anything for the chance to work hard and succeed, but cannot afford the cost of entry; the young people who gave everything, and are left jobless and in debt.

What happens to the American Dream deferred? The UN internship auction—whatever it may actually entail—is in the end a good thing, because it made plain a system of privilege and bias few want to acknowledge. Economic discrimination is often not visible. Nor are the people it leaves behind.

What a relief it would be if every unpaid internship were an auction—if instead of a vague line about how the intern must "cover their own costs," the organization would tally up those costs and see who is able to pay them. The rest of us could watch, from the sidelines, as bias long denied plays out in public, as wealth morphs into merit before our eyes. Let them do their bidding in the open, and show us what it costs to succeed.

—Originally published May 4, 2013

Survival Is Not an Aspiration

On June 12, 2013, Low Pay Is Not Okay, a group fighting to raise wages for fast food workers, released a video criticizing a budgeting guide created by McDonald's. The guide showed that McDonald's workers cannot survive on a McDonald's salary. Aside from including dubious figures—$20 a month for health care, $0 for heating—the guide left out essentials like child care, food, and clothing. Low Pay Is Not Okay noted that even by McDonald's calculations, workers would need at least $15 per hour to make ends meet. The video went viral, and the guide was widely criticized.

But some argued that the guide was reasonable. "When I lived in St. Louis, my roommate and I each paid $425 per month [in rent]," wrote the *Washington Post*'s Timothy B. Lee, ignoring that St. Louis fast food workers are on strike because they cannot afford to live on their current wages.

He praised the guide for "offering practical advice on how to live on a modest income," a sentiment echoed by *Mother Jones's* Kevin Drum, who deemed it "an extremely conventional collection of good financial advice."

Defenders of the McDonald's budget use the same word to describe it: *realistic*. (Both Drum and Lee use this term.) The logic is that if people can literally survive on minimum wage—that is, not drop dead—then their wages are justified. Ignored in the plea for realism is the day-to-day reality of McDonald's workers—not whether they can live, but how. In one of the wealthiest countries in the world, privation should not come with the job description, and survival should not be an aspiration.

"Worrying about the future is the hardest part, because at $7.25, I don't have a future," wrote Stephanie Sanders, a McDonald's worker, in an essay for the *Milwaukee Journal-Sentinel*. Like many fast food workers, Sanders is an adult who never thought she would end up in the food service industry. While the unemployment rate in America has remained largely steady in 2013, the underemployment rate has soared, and Sanders, a former saleswoman, has found herself trapped. Her temporary job has become a permanent sentence.

As economic analyst Robert Reich observes, "Being wealthy in America today means not having to come across anyone who isn't." For the last decade, the American media have railed against the "obesity crisis," blaming fast food outlets for poor public health. That the people who prepare this food lack the money to eat or feed their children—"We all worry about going hungry or ending up homeless," writes Sanders—attracts far less outrage.

Journalist Mark Oppenheimer calls the elite Americans obsessed with locally grown and organic food "the new Puritans"—and like the old Puritans, they tend to have a Calvinist take on those less fortunate. "Most of the middle-class 'liberal' parents I know have allowed lifestyle decisions about what they wear, eat, and drive to entirely replace a more ambitious program for bettering society," he writes. The plight of the McDonald's worker, like McDonald's itself, is seen as outside their purview.

The Myth of Upward Mobility

This lapse in priorities—in which things we buy are thought to be morally superior to people who sell them—parallels a change in the American perception of employment and social status. Jobs are no longer jobs but symbolic positions, indicative of where you come from and determinative of where you go.

The McDonald's worker, the argument goes, deserves what

> *The job you work increasingly reflects the money you already had.*

she gets because she is a McDonald's worker. The professional, it is said, deserves her success because she is a professional. But over the last decade, the barriers to entry for white-collar professions have dramatically increased while the pathways out of poverty have eroded. The job you work increasingly reflects the money you already had.

Upward mobility was once the hallmark of the American Dream. Downward wages have made that dream unachievable for Americans born poor. One McDonald's worker, Devonte Yates, is struggling to complete an associate's degree in criminal justice—the path to a stable life through education so often recommended. But Yates can barely buy food on McDonald's wages, much less pay his tuition.

Education is a luxury the minimum wage worker cannot afford. This message is passed on to their children. "My son is about to graduate from kindergarten, and I don't even have enough money to get his cap and gown, and that's only $20," says McDonald's worker Carman Iverson.

While many service workers live in poverty, well-off and well-educated professional workers increasingly find themselves working for poverty wages or for nothing at all. *The Atlantic* is one of many media outlets that covered the plight of the underpaid McDonald's worker—while simultaneously refusing to pay many of their own writers. Young Americans seeking full-time employment tend to find their options limited to two paths: one of low-status, low-paying temp jobs emblematic of poverty; another of high-status, low-paying temp jobs emblematic of wealth. America is not only a nation of temporary employees—the Walmart worker on a fixed-day contract, the immigrant struggling for a day's pay in a makeshift "temp town"—but of temporary jobs: intern, adjunct, fellow.

Like their counterparts in the service industry, these short-term prestige positions frequently offer no benefits, no health care, and in the case of the intern, no salary. They require that you have the money to move to switch jobs year after year—impossible for many, but easy for those with cash to spare. In the end, college graduates who trained for white-collar professions often cannot afford to take them, and end up, instead, working at a place like McDonald's.

Post-recession America runs on a contingency economy based on prestige and privation. The great commonality is that few are paid enough to live instead of simply survive.

Poverty Is Lost Potential

On July 20, 2013, the journalist Helen Thomas died at age ninety-two. Thomas was a seminal Washington reporter who covered every president since John F. Kennedy, but she came from humble means. Her father, an immigrant from Lebanon, was illiterate, but he encouraged her to get an education. She earned a BA in English from Wayne State University in her native Detroit. She moved to Washington, D.C., and worked as a waitress—one could once afford to live in D.C. on a waitress's salary—and then got a clerical job at the *Washington Daily News,* which led to a job with the United Press Service.

Helen Thomas worked her way up from the bottom. She did not buy her opportunities, because exorbitant journalism schools and unpaid internships did not exist. Her time in the service industry was not perceived as indicative of her abilities or her future path.

Today, a reporter of Thomas's modest background is out of luck. Journalist David Dennis argues that requiring unpaid internships shuts out voices from poor communities by denying those who hail from them the ability to work: "Opinions or perspectives reflecting my own come few and far between. How many journalists can say they have first-hand knowledge of the mentality of someone from the inner-city? Many of these voices have been muted just because they simply can't navigate the landscape of privilege that most modern journalism encourages."

Mistaking wealth for virtue is a cruelty of our time. By treating poverty as inevitable for parts of the population, and giving impoverished workers no means to rise out of it, America deprives not only them but society as a whole. Talented and hardworking people are denied the ability to contribute, and society is denied the benefits of their gifts. Poverty is not a character flaw. Poverty is not emblematic of intelligence. Poverty is lost potential, unheard contributions, silenced voices.

Working at McDonald's is not indicative of all a person can accomplish, nor should it be a sentence to limited opportunity. The service industry is increasingly where Americans end up, as pre-recession jobs are replaced with part-time, poverty-wage work. If temporary jobs are a permanent problem, we need to improve their conditions—along with those of the white-collar jobs to which many aspire but cannot afford to take.

—*Originally published July 22, 2013*

Zero-Opportunity Employers

On September 1, 2013, Margaret Mary Vojtko, an eighty-three-year-old adjunct professor at Duquesne University, died in abject poverty. Professor Vojtko taught French at Duquesne for twenty-five years. She received up to $3,500 per course and made an annual salary of less than $10,000. This is standard pay for adjuncts, who comprise 76 percent of the teaching workforce of tertiary institutions in the United States (tenure and tenure-track professors make up a mere 24 percent) and receive an average $2,700 per course.

Like most adjuncts, Professor Vojtko received no health care or benefits. When she was diagnosed with cancer, she could not pay her bills. She took a second job in a fast food restaurant and slept in her office until the university threw her out. In the spring of 2013, Duquesne fired her for no longer being "effective."

Living in poverty, dying of cancer, Professor Vojtko never missed a day of class. Vojtko's story is unique neither to adjuncts, who shared their own stories of privation on Twitter under the hashtag IAmMargaretMary, nor to other American workers. In the post-employment economy, full-time jobs are parceled into low-wage contract labor, entry-level jobs turn into internships, salaries are paid in exposure, and dignity succumbs to desperation.

On August 28, 2013, America celebrated the fiftieth anniversary of the March on Washington for Jobs and Freedom. Most Americans associate the march with Martin Luther King Jr.'s "I Have a Dream" speech and call for racial harmony. They remember half of the targeted "twin evils" of racism and economic deprivation.

They remember the freedom, and forget the jobs. But the two are inseparable.

"If a man doesn't have a job or an income, he has neither life nor liberty nor the possibility for the pursuit of happiness. He merely exists," King proclaimed in 1968. Economic opportunity, he argued, is essential to human rights.

How far we have fallen today, when survival is sold as an aspiration to the poor. How facile our claims of "equal opportunity" when the content of one's character is eclipsed by the content of one's wallet. Citizens struggling to pull themselves up—through education, through hard work—sink back down, into debt from student loans, into desperation from appeasing the few and powerful who defaulted on their future. America has abandoned any pretense of social mobility. In 2012, the income gap between the wealthiest 1 percent and the rest of America passed the record set in 1927, at the onset of the Great Depression. Forty percent of Americans now make less than minimum wage workers did in 1968, the year King died.

The Hidden Hand...

The problem in America is not that there are no jobs. It is that jobs are not paying.

America is becoming a nation of zero-opportunity employers, in which certain occupations are locked into a terrible pay rate for no valid reason, and certain groups—minorities, the poor, and increasingly, the middle class—are locked out of professions because they cannot buy their way in.

Why was Margaret Mary Vojtko, an experienced teacher who did the same work as a tenured professor, making less than $10,000? Because her university refused to pay her more than $10,000. Why is Deirdre Cunningham, a New York woman who works two jobs as a bank teller and a sales associate, living in a homeless shelter? Because her employers refuse to pay her enough to live anywhere else. Cunningham's plight

In the post-employment economy, full-time jobs are parceled into low-wage contract labor, entry-level jobs turn into internships, salaries are paid in exposure, and dignity succumbs to desperation.

is common: 28 percent of homeless families include at least one working adult.

During the recession, American companies found an effective new way to boost profits. It was called "not paying people." "Not paying people" tends to be justified in two ways: a fake crisis ("Unfortunately, we can't afford to pay you at this time . . .") or a false promise ("Working for nearly nothing now will get you a good job later").

In reality, profits are soaring and poorly compensated labor tends to lead to more poorly compensated labor. Zero-opportunity employers are refusing to pay people because they can get away with it. The social contract does not apply to contract workers—and in 2013, that is increasingly what Americans are.

One can see the truth of King's equation of income and rights in the powerlessness of low-wage workers to change their situation. Wages are not corresponding to demand or credentials. In a post-employment economy, wages are both arbitrary and fixed.

Institutionalized Exploitation

People who justify poverty wages tend to make two claims. The first is that desirable jobs have a surplus of applicants so their pay is inherently less. In 2013, every job has a surplus of applicants, yet the pay for some jobs—Wall Street bankers—rises while the pay for other jobs stagnates or disappears.

The second claim is that low-wage workers are easily

replaceable and offer no benefit to society. This is the argument aimed at service workers, who are on strike because they make so little they cannot afford food or rent.

Putting aside that anyone working full-time should be able to survive on their income, and that service workers deserve the same respect as any employee, this argument falls flat because educated professionals whose work offers tremendous benefit to society are also poorly paid.

Teaching, nursing, social work, child care, and other "pink collar" professions do not pay poorly because, as *Slate*'s Hanna Rosin argues, women "flock to less prestigious jobs," but because jobs are considered less prestigious when they are worked by women. The jobs are not worth less—but the people who work them are supposed to be.

Although zero-opportunity employers disproportionately hurt women and minorities, everyone suffers in an economy that does not value workers. "I didn't risk my life in Afghanistan so I could come back and watch people go hungry in America," writes Jason Kirell, a thirty-five-year-old veteran who is on food stamps. "I certainly didn't risk it so I could come back and go hungry." He notes that it is common for military wives to subsist on food stamps while their husbands work overseas and for veterans to end up on food stamps upon their return.

The Americans who serve their country the most are paid the least and treated the worst. As Kirell detailed his plight, House Republicans voted to cut the nation's food stamp program by $40 billion.

Into the Abyss

In America, there is little chance at a reversal of fortune for those less fortunate. Poverty is a sentence for the crime of existing. Poverty is a denial of rights sold as a character flaw.

There are two common responses to the plight of the low-wage worker. The first is "That's just the way things are," a response which serves both to derail empathy and deter people from imagining the way things could be.

The second is "But it worked out for me." This is the refrain of the tenured to the adjunct, the staffer to the freelancer, the rich to the poor: "But it worked out for me; the system is fine, it worked out for me."

The problem is that in an economy of falling wages and eroded safety nets, there is a very fine line between "you" and "me."

People not only fall through the cracks, they live in the cracks as a full-time occupation. The view from the cracks is a lot clearer than the view from above. When you look down on people, they stop being people. But when you watch from below, you see how easy it is to fall.

Personal success does not excuse systematic exploitation. "That's just the way things are" does not explain widespread suffering. Ask why things are the way they are, why things are not working out for working Americans.

And when they do not give you an answer? Start demanding one.

—Originally published September 23, 2013

A Government Shutdown, a
Social Breakdown

I n December 1995, the United States government shut down for twenty-one days, ending a year marked by violent fringe politics—the Oklahoma City bombings, the Unabomber manifesto—and the televised train wreck of the O. J. Simpson trial. In 1995, Americans watched fistfight talk shows and government conspiracy dramas and sitcoms about the pointlessness of living. The shutdown seemed of a piece with the era, idiocy ascended to a higher plane.

We rolled our eyes and waited it out. Because in 1995, when the government shut down, odds seemed good it would come back.

Americans tend to remember the 1990s through a soft flannel gauze—the peacetime complacency, the political correctness, the jobs—but they were garish, paranoid times. Today the 1990s feel like a dream only because the nightmare they created became ordinary. In the decade to come, the tabloid would become gospel, the social fabric sewn from the lunatic fringe. Radical polarization became rote. America went crazy and never went back.

The political tabloidization of the 1990s—a decade-long parade of sex scandals filling time between the Cold War and the War on Terror—seems like the indulgence of a nation that, in the absence of an obvious crisis, made themselves their own.

But a crisis was always there—only it was to be repackaged, not solved. Belying the vitriolic partisanship of the 1990s was a uniform agreement to gut social services to the sick and the poor. The impoverished were portrayed as a privileged class siphoning state resources at their leisure.

This argument dates back to President Reagan's denouncement of so-called "welfare queens"—and the bedrock for it was laid well before that—but it was the 1990s when it found mainstream appeal. In 1996, President Clinton signed the Personal Responsibility and Work Opportunity Act—a reform that limited welfare benefits—to the approval of most Democrats and Republicans.

It is easy to make public services seem optional when people feel like they have options. In the mid-1990s, when the economy was flourishing and unemployment was falling, you could tell someone to "go get a job" and it was possible they might actually find one.

This advice did nothing to mend the structural inequalities that underlaid the plight of the poor. But it was an argument that seemed less callous, less obviously destructive, than it does today. Today the advice remains the same—

but the options for ordinary Americans have dramatically changed.

Abdicating the Imaginary Throne of the "Welfare Queen"

American ideology has long tilted between individualism and Calvinism. What happened to you was either supposed to be in your control—the "pull yourself up by your bootstraps" approach—or divinely arbitrated. You either jumped, or you were meant to fall.

Claims you were pushed, or you were born so far down you could not climb up, were dismissed as excuses of the lazy. This is the way many saw their world before it collapsed.

By the end of the 1990s, the U.S. unemployment rate had reached a twenty-five-year low of 3.8 percent, and a mere 6.1 percent of Americans relied on food stamps. Today a record 15 out of every 100 Americans need food stamps, and 45 percent of all infants born in the United States are served by the Women, Infants, and Children program (WIC), which provides formula and vouchers for healthy food.

To be eligible for WIC, one's income must be below 185 percent of the U.S. poverty income. A near majority of American households now meet this criterion, despite the unemployment rate hovering at 7.3 percent.

The reason for this is that jobs have stopped paying. Homeless people are working two jobs. Walmart and McDonald's employees frequently receive federal assistance. Military wives survive on food stamps, and their husbands survive on them when they come home. The number of Americans on the Supplemental Nutrition Assistance Program has risen 70 percent since 2008 and shows no sign of stopping.

The reign of the "welfare queen" is finally over, because her true identity has been revealed. We are all the welfare queen, and we are abdicating her imaginary throne. The stigma of public assistance is slowly subsiding—not through a surge of compassion, but through an increase in desperation.

People are more likely to condemn people on government assistance when they do not know any of them personally. It is becoming less and less likely that this is the case.

The New American Dream

Americans are not as divided as they seem. We agree on guns—90 percent of Americans support expanded background checks on gun owners—and we largely agree on health care. Only one-third of Americans support repealing, defunding, or delaying President Obama's health care law. These numbers decrease when the law is called by its name, the Affordable Care Act, instead of Obamacare. Seventy-two percent of Americans agree that there should not be a government shutdown.

But our opinion does not matter. We are passive subjects, held hostage to a vindictive minority divorced from public will.

Political scientist Daniel Drezner has noted that the government shutdown has no real precedent in American history. "The material interests on the GOP side appear to have zero influence over their party," he writes, noting the failure of the long-standing American tradition of pluralism. "Now it's the ideological interests that are ascendant— and this poses enormous challenges to the American body politic."

Rule by ideology is far more dangerous than it was in the 1990s, because this shutdown takes place in extreme economic vulnerability. Like the current shutdown, the current unemployment crisis has no precedent. The great lesson of the past decade was that any employee can be arbitrarily deemed nonessential or unworthy of pay.

In an era when entry-level jobs become unpaid internships and full-time jobs turn into contingency labor, it is easy to imagine the cuts from the sequester becoming permanent. Shutdown furloughs may turn into layoffs, as elected officials, now marketing survival as the new American Dream, will assure us we did fine without them.

The nonessential worker is the archetypal hire. Our worst-case scenarios are simply scenarios.

Socioeconomic Astigmatism

In 1964, President Lyndon B. Johnson declared a War on Poverty. Over the next half century, that war turned into a war on the poor. This war was once disguised as "compassionate conservatism" and debated with words like "responsibility" and "opportunity."

Compassionate conservatism assumed that we could

take care of ourselves so we did not need to take care of each other. It was an attractive concept, simultaneously exalting the successes of America while relieving the individual of responsibility for those whom it failed. Many good people believed in it.

Today the attack on the poor is no longer cloaked in ideology—it is ideology itself. This ideology is not shared by most Americans, but by those seeking to transform the Republican Party into, as former GOP operative Mike Lofgren describes it, "an apocalyptic cult, or one of the intensely ideological authoritarian parties of 20th century Europe."

These are the people who have decided that poor children should be denied food as a result of elected officials wanting poor people to have health care.

The government shutdown only formalizes the dysfunction that has been hurting ordinary Americans for decades. It is not a political shutdown but a social breakdown. Fixing it requires a reassessment of value—and values.

When wealth is passed off as merit, bad luck is seen as bad character. This is how ideologues justify punishing the sick and the poor. But poverty is neither a crime nor a character flaw. Stigmatize those who let people die, not those who struggle to live.

—Originally published October 4, 2013

The Men Who Set
Themselves on Fire

On October 4, a man poured gasoline over his body and set himself on fire in Washington, D.C. He committed suicide in the National Mall, the open-air park surrounded by national museums and monuments, now closed due to the government shutdown.

Witnesses say he had set up a tripod to film his self-immolation. They say that before he killed himself he was yelling about voting rights. The man on fire was black. In June, the U.S. Supreme Court struck down key parts of the Voting Rights Act, proclaiming racial discrimination a thing of the past.

Now it is the government that is struck down, paralyzed by vindictive partisanship while its most vulnerable citizens suffer.

As I write this, no one knows who the man was or why he did it. But his act is not unique. He joins a long list of men who have self-immolated since the global financial collapse and subsequent austerity. Around the world, men are setting themselves on fire because they cannot find work.

This is happening in the world's richest and poorest nations, in its allegedly stable democracies and in its most ruthless dictatorships. The men who do this are young and old, of all races and religions, united only by their joblessness and their despair.

In the U.K., an unemployed forty-eight-year-old man set himself on fire outside a job center after not receiving a needed payment. In Morocco, a group of young law students, belonging to a group called Unemployed Graduates, set themselves on fire after not finding work. In Spain, a man burned himself alive because he did not have enough money for food. In Greece, a fifty-five-year-old man set himself on fire after screaming that he was in debt. In Bulgaria, several unemployed men self-immolated after condemning graft and corruption. In France, over a dozen people—both French nationals and immigrants, from different occupations and social classes—set themselves on fire because they could not find jobs.

This is a partial list. Unemployed men have self-immolated in Germany, Iraq, Jordan, China, Algeria, Tunisia, Egypt, and elsewhere. Many cases receive little media attention.

The week before the man burned himself alive on the National Mall, a man in a business suit tried to set himself on fire in Houston, Texas, after telling passersby that he could not find a job. The case did not make the national news. The government shut down four days later, pushing another 800,000 people out of work.

It's the Austerity, Stupid

Unemployment is not only the loss of a job. It is the loss of dignity. It is the loss of the present and, over time, the ability to imagine a future. It is hopelessness and shame, an open struggle everyone witnesses but pretends not to see. It is a social and political crisis we tell a man to solve, and blame him when he cannot.

When you are unemployed, your past is dismissed as unworthy. Your future is denied. Self-immolation is making yourself, in the moment, matter.

The most famous recent case of an unemployed man setting himself on fire was Mohamed Bouazizi, the Tunisian street vendor whose actions are said to have spurred the Arab Spring revolutions. When Bouazizi killed himself in December 2010, the youth unemployment rate was 30 percent in Tunisia and 25 percent in Egypt, where uprisings quickly followed.

In Spain, three years later, youth unemployment is 57 percent. In Greece, it is 64 percent. The youth unemployment rate is 23.5 percent for the combined European Union and 16 percent for the United States, a statistic which does not take into account the millions whose jobs do not pay enough to take them out of poverty. The youth unemployment rates of Western nations now mirror or surpass those of the Arab world before the uprisings.

When Bouazizi self-immolated, the case was initially covered as an act of economic desperation. Only after it triggered a mass outcry was it acknowledged as a political statement, a final stand against decades of corruption and autocracy. It is pointless to ask whether the self-immolation of an unemployed man is an economic or political act: the two are inseparable.

The knowledge of their inseparability is in part what inspires these men to act. One can call it austerity or one can call it apathy, but the end result is that states are letting their citizens die—slowly and silently in poverty, or publicly in flame.

As journalist Kevin Drum observes, in every previous recession, government spending rose. In this recession, they cut benefits, food stamps, jobs. They cut and blame us when we bleed.

In authoritarian states ruled by tyrants, in democracies allegedly ruled by law, we find the same result: hardworking people let down by the systems that are supposed to support them. When the most you can ask from your society is that it will spare you, you have no society of which to speak.

The Suffering Silent

"Rome wasn't built in a day," the saying goes. "But it was burned in one."

Today Rome does not burn—its stocks continue to rise, its wealthy continue to profit. Rome does not burn. Only its victims do.

For every person who sets himself on fire there are millions suffering in silence. For every person who becomes a symbol, there are millions who watch quietly, in shock and resignation, resigned to our shock, shocked by our deference.

Self-immolation has long been an act of protest against corrupt and tyrannical rule: Tibetans against the Chinese, Czechoslovakians against the Soviets. The difference between these acts of protest and the unemployed men on fire is that today we are not sure who is in charge.

The U.S. government, after all, cannot even govern itself. State attempts at improving social welfare are trumped not by public will or political disagreement but by what appears to be a pre-planned, funded attempt by fringe conservatives to shut the government down.

In every country with massive unemployment—which is, increasingly, every country—citizens see the loss of a functioning social contract, and the apathy with which that loss is received.

We do not know the identity of the man on fire. We do not know what prompted him to kill himself in open view in the nation's capital. We know he was a man who died. That should be enough. In every act of agony, that should be enough.

—*Originally published October 7, 2013*

Charity Is Not a
Substitute for Justice

On November 15, thousands of people in San Francisco worked together to make an ailing child's wish come true. Miles Scott, a five-year-old boy recovering from leukemia, dreamed of becoming "Batkid." At the behest of the Make-a-Wish Foundation, a charity that grants the wishes of children with life-threatening illnesses, San Franciscans staged an elaborate series of events for Scott and his family. He rode in the Batmobile, rescued a damsel in distress, and received national press coverage and a personal message from President Barack Obama.

The public effort for Scott shows what a difference kindness and compassion can make for a family in need. But one of the reasons the Batkid outreach was so moving is that it is such a rare occurrence.

In an era where bad luck is mistaken for bad character, the plight of those worse off tends to be ignored or portrayed as a perverse form of retribution. Poverty becomes both a crime and its own punishment, even for children. In many U.S. schools, a child who cannot come up with lunch money is expected to go hungry. In Texas, a twelve-year-old's lunch was thrown in the trash because he could not come up with the 30 cents to pay for it.

The outreach for Batkid was celebrated as a triumph of the human spirit. But what it demonstrated is how much better society could be if generosity were consistently applied toward all, instead of concentrated into brief celebratory affairs.

"Charity is no substitute for justice withheld," Saint Augustine once declared. This is painfully clear in San Francisco and its surrounding area, home to some of the highest income inequality in the country.

"San Francisco itself is turning into a private, exclusive club," noted Anisse Gross in *The New Yorker*. "The city, long reputed as a haven for provocateurs and cultural innovators, has quickly transformed into a playground for the rich, where tech money sends rental prices soaring as the less fortunate tenants battle it out with the rent board."

As journalist Alyssa Rosenberg argues, Batkid was supported by the tech community, who saw the event as a way to indulge in their own superhero fantasies. Yet the broader message of the tech community is that most children do not deserve to be saved. Silicon Valley is a region of "masters and servants," where homelessness has increased 8 percent, as salaries skyrocket. A proposal for Silicon Valley to secede and therefore deny taxpayer money to social programs benefiting low-income residents, including children, was met by many with approval.

Charity as a Substitute

Charity, as a supplement to justice, should be applauded. But charity as a substitute for justice is neither charity nor justice. It is cruelty.

The same week that the nation cheered a charitable effort to make one child's wish come true, the largest employer in the U.S. held a charity drive for some of its own workers. Walmart, whose six heirs to the company fortune have as much wealth as the bottom 42 percent of Americans, pays its workers salaries so low that many qualify for food stamps.

The costs are then transferred to taxpayers. A report by the House Committee on Education and the Workforce estimated that one Walmart Supercenter employing three hundred workers could cost taxpayers at least $904,000 annually.

Yet instead of raising salaries to allow employees to live above the dole, Walmart encourages charity—a common panacea to social plight. Universities employing adjunct professors, who are also paid below poverty wages, have held similar food drives for their employees.

In September, Margaret Mary Vojtko, a Duquesne University professor, who had worked at the school for twenty-five years, died in abject poverty with an annual salary of less than $10,000. Responding to accusations of callousness, Duquesne noted that they had offered Vojtko charity, such as an offer to fix her furnace. A *Slate* article promising the "real story" of Vojtko argued that she brought her troubles upon herself by refusing Duquesne's gifts while working with a growing movement of adjuncts attempting to unionize.

In other words, Vojtko refused charity while pursuing justice. This is not a position to condemn.

Fiscal stability that relies on gifts is not stability. It is a guarantee of insecurity: income based not on work but on whim. Capricious generosity is not a replacement for a living wage, nor is it a basis for a functioning society. Charity is no substitute for justice.

Living on a Gamble

In rural Missouri, there is a store called Nick's Gun and Pawn. Locals can trade their weapons for household items, or vice versa. It is one of many examples of one of the most overlooked stories in the great recession: the explosion of pawnshops and payday loan outlets throughout the U.S. Between 2009 and 2011, the rate of Americans using high-cost nonbank credit soared to 14 percent, and included a rise in population segments once considered economically advantaged, but now unable to afford daily needs.

Pawnshops and payday loans are the flip side of the United States' turn to charity over justice. Both phenomena speak to a seemingly permanent impermanence: the replacement of a reliable salary for hard work, with high-cost gambles and unpredictable donations.

In much of the U.S., possessions are not things you own. They are disaster protection, what you trade to survive. The consequences are not only material but psychological. When you are constantly gambling, the future comes to look like a bad bet.

Journalist Gillian Tett notes that poorer Americans, living check to check, are "more likely to perceive the future as a chaotic series of short-term cycles." When people are expected to work unpaid for the promise of work, the advantage goes to those immune from the hustle: the owners over the renters, the salaried over the contingent. Attempts to ensure stability and independence for citizens—such as affordable health care—are decried as government "charity" while corporate charity is proffered as a substitute for a living wage.

"We don't plan long-term because if we do, we'll just get our hearts broken," wrote Linda Walther Tirado, a blogger who described her own struggle with poverty in a much circulated essay. "It's best not to hope. You just take what you can get as you spot it."

"Taking what you can get" is also the path pursued by corporations and people who prefer cheap acts of charity to long-term investments in justice. It is a path that encourages citizens to depend on arbitrary generosity while decrying stable programs that help people through tough times. It trades in racial stereotypes, portraying the poor as lazy, violent, and "undeserving" of either assistance or the benefit of the doubt.

On November 23, East Saint Louis, an impoverished

city with a high rate of gun violence, offered a trade to city residents: bring in your gun and receive a $100 gift certificate at a local grocery store. At 9:00 A.M. a long line had formed of residents with guns in hands. Within ten minutes, $10,000 of grocery store gift cards had been given away.

Some were surprised by the outcome. They should not have been. Ours is an economy of survival. Violence is often the last resort for people out of options. When presented with options, they chose food.

Charity, for the giver, is the trade of cash for a moral fix. As the Make-a-Wish showed, charity can be beautiful. But it is an investment in the present, not the future. If you value the future—if you value a society where people can imagine their future—work for justice.

—*Originally published December 6, 2013*

The Unaffordable Baby Boomer Dream

On February 12, President Obama declared that his administration was taking steps to address a crisis in American higher education: the skyrocketing cost of tuition coupled with the significant unemployment rate for recent college graduates. He announced the creation of a College Scorecard that would rate schools based on "simple criteria: where you can get the most bang for your educational buck."

Released online the next day, the College Scorecard drew criticism from education experts. Most noted that it was missing important information on employment rates and income levels for graduates of particular schools. But Harvard president Drew Gilpin Faust had a different critique. After stating that the point of a college degree was not a "first job" but "a lifetime of citizenship, opportunity, growth and change," she recounted her own experience.

She wrote in a letter to *The New York Times*:

I graduated from Bryn Mawr College in 1968, and my first job was working for the Department of Housing and Urban Development. My starting salary was low, but I was inspired by the civil rights movement and the War on Poverty to regard public service as an important calling. I went on to graduate school, joined the faculty at the University of Pennsylvania and ultimately became the president of Harvard University. Should Bryn Mawr have been judged based on what I was paid in my first year at HUD?

Faust's is an inspiring tale—and one beyond the comprehension of most young graduates in America today. "Don't trust the boomers!" warned Paul Campos in a 2012 article on the misguided advice the elder generation peddles to their underemployed, debt-ridden progeny—including gems like "higher education is always worth the price" and "internships lead to jobs"—and Faust's rebuke proves him right.

What is most remarkable about Faust's career is not its culmination in the Harvard presidency, but the system of accessibility and opportunity that allowed her to pursue it. Her life story is a eulogy for an America of the past.

Unpaid Labor

Let's review what life was like for an American of Faust's generation. In 1968, when Faust graduated from Bryn Mawr, tuition and board at a four-year private university cost an average of $2,545. As the scion of a wealthy political family, it is doubtful Faust had to worry about affording tuition, but neither did most members of her generation, since the cost of attending college was relatively low. Today, Bryn Mawr costs $53,040 per year—more than the American median household income.

In 1968, $2,545 was about the most you could expect to pay for college—most schools cost half as much, and many public universities were still free. Faust's generation graduated with little to no debt, unlike today's university graduate, who owes an average of $27,000. After graduating, Faust decided to pursue a life of public service and got a job—an actual, paying job, right out of college—with the Department of Housing and Urban Development.

The hippie movement reached its height in 1968, but it is perhaps difficult for the modern mind to comprehend the desire to "turn on, tune in, and drop out" when such a novel option as post-college employment was available. Today's graduate seeking a career in government often winds up in an internship, where they work full-time for little to no pay.

In her article "The Age of the Permanent Intern," journalist Hannah Seligson describes Jessica, a full-time intern at the Woodrow Wilson International Center for Scholars, who was paid $4.35 an hour during her ten-month tenure. Despite simultaneously shelling out $50,000 per year for a graduate degree at American University, Jessica says she felt lucky, because without internships and an MA she had no chance at an entry-level job. Seligson reflects: "Talking to her, I wonder: When did 'lucky' become working for below minimum wage for months on end?"

Seligson is right: luck does not have much to do with it. In order to work the internship that is a requirement for entry in many fields, a young graduate requires substantial financial support as well as previous unpaid experience. "Almost none of the kids I meet in Washington these days even had boring menial high-school jobs working in a drugstore or waiting tables; they were doing 'enriching' internships or academic programs," writes pundit Megan McArdle.

Participation in these programs and internships is often dependent on personal wealth, resulting in a system of privilege that replicates itself over generations. McArdle compares America's eroded meritocracy to imperial China, noting that "the people entering journalism, or finance, or consulting, or any other 'elite' profession, are increasingly the children of the children of those who rocketed to prosperity through the postwar education system. A window that opened is closing."

"Currency" Counts

But for Faust's baby boomer generation, the window was open, the opportunities there. Following the paid position she took after her four years of inexpensive college, Faust went on to get a PhD. She graduated in 1975, a year when over half of history PhD's could expect to find a job in their chosen field, and immediately landed a teaching position at the same university where she studied.

Today, only 42.6 percent of history PhD's are employed

upon graduation, and few in academia. Those who find jobs in higher education often work as low-paid adjuncts—a category that was miniscule in 1975, but now makes up roughly 70 percent of American faculty. Like internships, adjunct positions are often necessary to advance professionally—but only the well-off can afford to work them without living in poverty or debt. The result is a professoriate of an increasingly uniform class background, much like the policy, finance, and journalism circles McArdle describes. Mobility is but a memory. "The life prospects of an American are more dependent on the income and education of his parents than in almost any other advanced country for which there is data," writes economist Joseph E. Stiglitz in an editorial aptly titled "Equal Opportunity, Our National Myth."

To understand the repercussions of the current system, it is worth taking a look at another woman born in 1947, the same year as Faust. A few weeks ago, a meme began circulating on Facebook: "Hillary Clinton wrote to NASA as a child inquiring how to be an astronaut," it said. "NASA replied that girls could not be astronauts. So she became Secretary of State."

The meme served as a reminder that opportunities in the 1960s were far more limited for minorities and women than now—a point Faust, Harvard's first female president, has noted. It also meant to serve as inspiration for those whose dreams have been denied. But while barriers based on race and gender have eased—to a degree, with still a long way to go—economic strictures have tightened, denying the dreams of a new generation.

One can argue that today the path to becoming an astronaut—one of the most notoriously difficult professions to enter—is more meritocratic for an individual of Clinton's middle-class background than the path to jobs in policy and other fields relying on upfront costs and nepotistic connections. Astronauts do not labor unpaid for years; the children of astronauts do not automatically become astronauts.

This is not to say that hardworking elites do not deserve their success, but that the greatest barrier to entry in many professions is financial, not intellectual. The ambition, hard work, and idealism of women like the young Hillary Clinton have no currency in today's system, because only one type of currency—hard currency—counts.

One wonders how many future politicians, journalists, academics, and leaders we are losing because they never have the chance to try. How many people from Hillary Clinton's middle-class background—or, for that matter, from Bill Clinton's rural poverty—can afford to tread the path of debt and unpaid labor required to succeed?

The "lifetime of citizenship, opportunity, growth and change" Drew Gilpin Faust extolled is something most Americans desire. But it is affordable only for a select few: the baby boomers who can buy their children opportunities as the system they created screws the rest.

—*Originally published February 26, 2013*

The Millennial Parent

have a friend who was the first in his family to go to college. He grew up poor in the rural Midwest and earned his BA from a top school in the region. But when the recession hit in the early 2000s, he could not find a job. He decided he needed more training and applied to graduate school. When Harvard accepted him, he was thrilled. Within one generation, his family's highest level of education went from a high school diploma to an Ivy League degree.

A Harvard education was supposed to provide opportunity. But with the degree came debt. Now in his early thirties with children of his own, my friend's social mobility has stalled. He wants his sons to have the same quality of education he did, and the professional advantages that come with it. But he does not see how this is possible. When his sons are old enough for college, he will still be paying back his own student loans. With wages stagnant and tuition fees well outpacing inflation, there is little chance he will be able to afford their education. His children will be back where he started. Mobility was a mirage.

"It kind of sickens me to think I might have to say to my kids, 'Hey, I went to Harvard but you can't,'" he said. "The whole thing is turned inside out. People imagine that you are supposed to build legacies around things like that, and instead they can't go there because I did." My friend is part of the so-called millennial generation: young adults born roughly between the late 1970s and the late 1990s. While the start and end dates of the millennial generation are up for debate—and the idea of inherent generational traits is dubious—people of this age group share an important quality. They have no adult experience in a functional economy.

Millennials are a favorite target of the media, who portray their economic plight as a character flaw. In a recent cover story, "The Me Me Me Generation," *Time* declared millennials "lazy, entitled narcissists who still live with their parents." While generational trolling spares no cohort, there was something particularly callous about *Time*'s depiction of young adults facing the worst economy since the Great Depression.

"Have you seen your intern on Rich Kids of Instagram?" *The Atlantic*'s Elspeth Reeve writes, noting that the *Time* portrayal seems modeled on privileged interns able to work for free. "If so, he or she is probably not the best guide to crafting the composite personality of a generation that fought three wars for you."

"Adults still living with their parents" is the classic

millennial trope. What is forgotten is how many millennials are parents themselves. As of 2010, 34 percent of U.S. residents aged 18 to 29 had children, according to one poll. Fewer than one-third of people in this age group have a full-time job. They have minimal savings and the highest student loan debt in recorded history. Most cannot afford cars, homes, health insurance, or other material goods once considered basic elements of life in the U.S. How can a generation that can barely stand on its feet be in charge of another generation's welfare?

Lack of Options

Being a responsible parent means planning for the future. But when many millennial parents look into the future, they see a void. Financial journalist Gillian Tett notes how economic polarization creates different cognitive maps. "If you were to ask wealthy Americans to visualize the future, they might well describe it as a carefully calibrated road along which they expect to travel," she writes. "But if you ask poorer Americans, who are scrambling from pay check to pay check, they are more likely to perceive the future as a chaotic series of short-term cycles."

Millennials are almost uniformly poorer Americans. Those who are financially secure tend to have family wealth. According to a 2012 Pew survey, 38 percent of millennials say their current financial situation is linked to their parents' financial situation. Millennials are chastised for leaning on elders, but the new rules of the economy demand it. Unpaid internships are often prerequisites to full-time jobs, and the ability to take them is based on money, not merit. Young adults who live off wealthy parents are the lucky few. They can envision a future because they can envision its purchase. Almost everyone else is locked out of the game.

Dependence may be the primary trait of the millennial generation, but it is a structural dependence, caused not by "laziness" or "narcissism" but by a lack of options or social mobility. For millennials much more than for the generations that immediately preceded them, the future is determined by the past. The son is indebted to the debt of the father.

When I ask millennial parents about how they see their children's future, they tell me they do not like to think about it. It is one thing to discover, as an adult, that the rules have been rewritten, that the job market will not recover, that you will scramble to survive. It is another to raise a child knowing that no matter how hard they work, how talented they are, how big they dream, they will not have opportunities—because in the new economy, opportunities are bought, not earned. You know this, but you cannot tell this to a child. The millennial parent is always Santa, always a little bit of a liar.

"Class Privilege"

Some may argue that the children of millennials do not have it so bad. Even if their parents cannot save enough to pay for college, surely they can apply for scholarships. But in the new economy, scholarships are increasingly reserved for the rich. According to a report from the New America Foundation, colleges give "merit aid" to wealthy students who can afford to pay nearly full tuition at the expense of aid to low-income students.

The goal is to increase the university's prestige by building an affluent student body. But the consequences for social mobility are so dire that the authors of the study argue for government intervention. "Federal action is needed to ensure that colleges continue to provide a gateway to opportunity, rather than perpetuating inequality by limiting college access to only those who are rich enough to be able to afford it," they write. The children of the millennials have been born into a United States of entrenched meritocracy— what Pierre Bourdieu called "the social alchemy that turns class privilege into merit." Success is allegedly based on competition, not background, but one must be prepared to pay to play.

"This reliance on un- or underpaid labor is part of a broader move to a 'privilege economy' instead of a merit economy—where who you know and who pays your bills can be far more important than talent," writes journalist Farai Chideya, noting that this system often locks out minorities. By charging more for a year's college tuition than the average median income, universities ensure that poor people stay poor while debt-ridden graduates join their ranks. By requiring unpaid internships, professions such as journalism ensure positions of influence will be filled only by

those who can pay for them. The cycle of privilege and privation continues.

The economy may seem bad now, but the true test will
come in the next two decades, when the children of the
"screwed generation" reap the meager harvest of their parents'
lost opportunities. Perhaps then we will return to the ideal
of equal opportunity because we will have witnessed the
long-term consequences of its erosion.

In the meantime, millennial parents surrender their
dreams in favor of survival. That is what a good parent does.
It is much harder to surrender a child's dreams as well.

—Originally published May 29, 2013

Mothers Are Not "Opting Out"— They Are Out of Options

Themothers of "The choice that is not really a choice" is one of the oldest tricks in parenting. Anticipating a tantrum or endless dawdling, the parent offers the child a limited set of options: "Would you like to wear the red shirt or the blue shirt? Would you like the carrots or the apple? It's your choice."

The child, being a child, feels empowered. He is the one in control; he gets to make the big decisions. But this deception only lasts for so long. Eventually the child grows older and starts to dream beyond his proscriptions. He realizes there are not only two options, but a world of dazzling variety. He demands to be part of this world, but his requests are denied. He realizes he never had options after all, but that choice itself was an illusion produced by the powerful.

If only his mother would realize the same.

On August 7, *The New York Times* ran an article called

"The Opt Out Generation Wants Back In"—a follow-up to a 2003 story about highly accomplished, well-educated American women who left the workforce to stay at home with their children. Ten years later, the mothers are seeking work that befits their abilities but most are unable to find it, causing them to question their original decision. *The New York Times* piece frames the mothers' misgivings as a result of questionable planning and poor marriage partners, paying mere lip service to the tremendous change in the economy over the past ten years. Whether to work or stay at home is presented as an option that has to do with personal fulfillment and child-rearing preferences, divorced from fiscal limitations.

But for nearly all women, from upper middle class to poor, the "choice" of whether to work is not a choice, but an economic bargain struck out of fear and necessity. Since 2008, the costs of childbirth, child care, health care, and education have soared, while wages have stagnated and full-time jobs have been supplanted by part-time, benefit-free contingency labor.

The media present a woman's fear of losing her career as the fear of losing herself. But the greatest fear of most mothers is not being able to provide for their children. Mothers with high-paying jobs go back to work to earn money for their kids. Married mothers with low-paying jobs quit to save money for their kids. Single mothers struggle to find work that pays enough to support their kids. Self-fulfillment is a low priority in an economy fueled by worker insecurity.

The assumed divide between mothers who work inside

and outside the home is presented as a war of priorities. But in an economy of high debt and sinking wages, nearly all mothers live on the edge. Choices made out of fear are not really choices. The illusion of choice is a way to blame mothers for an economic system rigged against them. There are no "mommy wars," only money wars—and almost everyone is losing.

Motherhood as a Financial Burden

Here is how raising a child in America has changed over the past decade. Between 2004 and 2010, the average out-of-pocket costs for childbirth rose fourfold, making American deliveries the costliest in the world. Two decades ago, insured American women, on average, paid nothing. Today the average out-of-pocket cost with insurance is $3,400, with many insured women paying much more, and uninsured mothers charged tens of thousands of dollars.

The average American woman begins the journey of motherhood paying off mountains of debt. One could argue there is indeed a "choice" at play: the hospitals and health insurance companies can choose to stop inflating prices, charging for unwanted procedures, or refusing to cover necessary ones.

But with the health insurance industry facing little accountability, the burden of "choice" reverts back to the mother. The skyrocketing cost of childbirth corresponds with the rise of the home birth movement, which, while appealing to some women for personal, noneconomic reasons, is also a way to try to dodge the hospital bill (for women with complicated deliveries, this "choice" is quickly curtailed). Like so many movements born in times of economic ruin, home birth is presented by the media as a lifestyle trend, a return to "natural living" much like the rise of bicycling (cannot afford a car), "shabby chic" (cannot afford new clothes or furniture), and gardening (cannot afford fresh produce).

Desperate or pragmatic economic decisions are rationalized with moral superiority. In the post-employment economy, "opting out" is often code for "cannot afford a job."

America is notorious for workplace policies that are unfriendly to mothers—we have among the shortest parental leave of any developed nation, with 40 percent of companies providing none at all. We also have among the world's most expensive child care (although our child care workers are paid a pittance). The average cost of day care is $11,666 per year, with the average cost in some states as high as $19,000. This means that young parents, still struggling to pay off their massive college loans, are also expected to pay day care costs equivalent to college tuition.

> *For nearly all women, from upper middle class to poor, the "choice" of whether to work is not a choice, but an economic bargain struck out of fear and necessity.*

Since the recession began, the cost of day care has soared while the U.S. median income collapsed, plummeting 7.3 percent. The average household makes $51,404 before taxes. A family with two children and two working parents could easily find over half of their income going to child care. For the average married mother of small children, it is often cheaper to stay home—even if she would prefer to be in the workforce. It is hard to "lean in" when you are priced out.

Regardless of their reasons, all mothers who stay home with children are penalized later by the perception that they "chose" to neglect their career. When they attempt to return to the workforce, their years at home are held against them, considered a "blank spot" on the résumé—a blank spot with a reason so obvious and laudable and often involuntary that it is sick we deride it as "choice."

Careers Are Not Pursued by Choice

Corporate feminists like Sheryl Sandberg frame female success as a matter of attitude. But it is really a matter of money—or the lack thereof. For all but the fortunate few, American motherhood is making sure you have enough lifeboats for your sinking ship. American motherhood is a cost-cutting, debt-dodging scramble somehow interpreted as a series of purposeful moves. American mothers are not "leaning in." American mothers are not "opting out." American mothers are barely hanging on.

Careers in this economy are not about choices. They are about structural constraints masquerading as choice. Being a mother is a structural constraint regardless of your economic position. Mothers pay a higher price in a collapsed economy, but that does not mean they should not demand change—both in institutions and perceptions.

Erasing stigma—whether of hardworking, impoverished single mothers branded as "lazy," or of wealthier mothers whose skills outside the home are downplayed and denied—does not cost a thing.

The irony of American motherhood is that the politicians and corporations who hold power do have a choice in how they treat mothers and their children. Yet they act as if they are held hostage to intractable policies and market forces, excusing the incompetence and corporate malfeasance that drain our households dry.

Mothers can emulate them and treat "choice" as an individual burden—or we can work together and push for accountability and reform. This option is not easy. But we are used to that.

—Originally published August 19, 2013

PART III

Race and Religion

The Wrong Kind of Caucasian

n 1901, a twenty-eight-year-old American named Leon Czolgosz assassinated President William McKinley. Czolgosz was born in America, but he was of Polish descent. After McKinley died, the American media blamed Polish immigrants. They were outsiders, foreigners, with a suspicious religion—Catholicism—and strange last names.

At a time when Eastern European immigrants were treated as inferior, Polish Americans feared they would be punished as a group for the terrible actions of an individual. "We feel the pain which this sad occurrence caused, not only in America, but throughout the whole world. All people are mourning, and it is caused by a maniac who is of our nationality," a Polish-American newspaper wrote in an anguished editorial.

It is a sentiment reminiscent of what Muslims and Chechens are writing—or Instagramming—today, after the revelation that Dzokhar and Tamerlan Tsarnaev, the suspects in the Boston Marathon bombings, are of Chechen descent. At this time, there is no evidence linking the Tsarnaev brothers to a broader movement in Chechnya, a war-torn federal republic in southern Russia. Neither of the brothers has ever lived there. The oldest, Tamerlan, was born in Russia and moved to the U.S. when he was sixteen. The youngest, Dzokhar, was born in Kyrgyzstan, moved to the U.S. when he was nine, and became a U.S. citizen in 2012.

Despite the Tsarnaevs' American upbringing, the media have presented their lives through a Chechen lens. Political strife in the North Caucasus, ignored by the press for years, has become the default rationale for a domestic crime.

"Did Boston carnage have its roots in Stalin's ruthless displacement of Muslims from Chechnya decades ago?" asked the *New York Daily News*, a question echoed by the *National Post*, the *Washington Post*, and other publications that refuse to see the Tsarnaevs as anything but walking symbols of age-old conflicts. Blame Stalin, the pundits cry, echoing the argument made every time something bad happens in the former Soviet Union. Blame Stalin, because we can pronounce that name. In one sense, this sentiment is not new. American Muslims have long had to deal with ignorance and prejudice in the aftermath of a terrorist attack. "Please don't be Muslims or Arabs," goes the refrain, as unnecessary demands for a public apology from Muslims emerge. This week made it clear that it is Muslims who are owed the apology. After wild speculation from CNN about a "dark-skinned suspect," on Thursday the *New York Post* published a cover photo falsely suggesting a Moroccan-American high school track star,

Salah Barhoun, was one of the bombers. "Jogging while Arab" has become the new "driving while black."

Later that Thursday, the FBI released photos of two young men wearing baseball caps—men who so resembled all-American frat boys that people joked they would be the target of "racial bro-filing." The men were Caucasian, so the speculation turned away from foreign terror and toward the excuses routinely made for white men who kill: mental illness, anti-government grudges, frustrations at home. The men were white and Caucasian—until the next day, when they became the wrong kind of Caucasian, and suddenly they were not so "white" after all.

Crucifying the Wrong Caucasian

Muslims face prejudice, but Muslims from the Caucasus face a particular kind of prejudice—the kind born of ignorance so great it perversely imbues everything with significance. "There is never interpretation, understanding and knowledge when there is no interest," Edward Said wrote in *Covering Islam,* and until this week, there was so little interest in and knowledge of the Caucasus that the ambassador of the Czech Republic felt compelled to issue a press release stating that the Czech Republic is not the same as Chechnya.

Knowing nothing of the Tsarnaevs' motives, and little about Chechens, the American media tore into Wikipedia and came back with stereotypes. The Tsarnaevs were stripped of their twenty-first-century American life and became symbols of a distant land, forever frozen in time. Journalist

Eliza Shapiro proclaimed that Tamerlan Tsarnaev was "named after a brutal warlord," despite the fact that Tamerlan, or Timur, is an ordinary first name in the Caucasus and Central Asia. Her claim is equivalent to saying a child named Nicholas must be named in honor of ruthless Russian tsar Nicholas I—an irony apparently lost on *New York Times* columnist Nicholas Kristof, who made a similar denouncement on Twitter (to his credit, Kristof quickly retracted the comment).

Other journalists found literary allusions, or rather, illusions. "They were playing the nihilists Arkady and Bazarov in Turgenev's *Fathers and Sons*," explained scholar Juan Cole, citing an 1862 Russian novel to explain the motives of a criminal whose Twitter account was full of American rap lyrics. One does not recall such use of literary devices to ascertain the motives of less exotic perpetrators, but who knows? Perhaps some ambitious analyst is plumbing the works of Faulkner to shed light on that Mississippi Elvis impersonator who tried to send ricin to President Obama.

Still others turned to social media as a gateway to the Chechen soul. Journalist Julia Ioffe—after explaining the Tsarnaevs through Tolstoy, Pushkin, and, of course, Stalin—cites the younger Tsarnaev's use of the Russian website VKontakte as proof of his inability to assimilate, then ranks the significance of his personal photos.

"The most revealing image of Dzhokhar is not the one of him hugging an African-American friend at his high school graduation, but the one of him sitting at a kitchen table with his arm around a guy his age who appears to be of Central Asian descent," she writes. "In front of them is a dish plov, a Central Asian dish of rice and meat, and a bottle of Ranch dressing." Again, it is difficult to imagine a journalist writing with such breathtaking arrogance—why is the Central Asian friend more "revealing" than the African-American one? What, exactly, are they "revealing" about the inner life of someone from a more familiar place?

One way to test whether you are reading a reasonable analysis of the Tsarnaev case—and yes, they exist—is to replace the word "Chechen" with another ethnicity. "I could always spot the Chechens in Vienna," writes journalist Oliver Bullough in *The New York Times*. "They were darker-haired than the Austrians; they dressed more snappily, like 1950s gangsters; they never had anything to do." Now substitute the word "Jews" for "Chechens." Minority-hunting in Vienna never ends well.

Demonizing an Ethnicity

It is easy to criticize the media, and after this disastrous week there is much to criticize. But the consequences of the casual racism launched at Chechens—and by association, all other Muslims from the former Soviet Union, who are rarely distinguished from one another by the public—are serious. By emphasizing the Tsarnaevs' ethnicity over their individual choices, and portraying that ethnicity as barbaric and violent, the media create a false image of a people destined by their names and their "culture of terror" to kill. There are no people in Chechnya, only symbols. There are no Chechen Americans, only threats.

Ethnicity is often used to justify violent behavior. But no ethnicity is inherently violent. Even if the Tsarnaevs aligned themselves with violent Chechen movements—and as of now, there is no evidence they did—treating Chechen ethnicity as the cause of the Boston violence is irresponsible.

One hundred years ago, the violent act of one Polish American caused a country to treat all Polish Americans with suspicion. Now, the Poles have become "white"—which is to say they are largely safe from the accusations of treason and murderous intent that ethnic groups deemed nonwhite routinely face. When a Polish American commits a crime, his ethnicity does not go on trial with him.

But this change is not a triumph for America. It is a tragedy that it happened to Poles then, and a greater tragedy that we have not learned our lesson and it happens still—to Hispanics, to Arabs, to Chechens, to any immigrant who comes here seeking refuge and finds prejudice instead.

"I respect this country, I love this country," the Tsarnaevs' uncle, Ruslan Tsarni, said in an emotional condemnation of his nephews. "This country which gives chance to everyone else to be treated as a human being."

Chechens and other Muslim immigrants from the former Soviet Union are human beings. They are not walking symbols of violent conflict. Do not look to a foreign country to explain a domestic crime. Look to the two men who did it—and judge them by what they have done, not from where their ancestors came.

—Originally published April 21, 2013

The Fallacy of the Phrase
"the Muslim World"

On September 12, 2012, the day after the attacks on the U.S. diplomatic missions in Egypt and Libya, *The New York Times* set out to explain what it called the "anguished relationship between the United States and the Muslim world." According to the *Times*, "the Muslim world" was prone to outbursts of violence, and the reaction to the fourteen-minute anti-Islam movie trailer *Innocence of Muslims* was both baffling and predictable. "Once again, Muslims were furious," wrote reporter Robert F. Worth, "and many in the West found themselves asking why Islam seems to routinely answer such desecrations with violence."

Other media outlets echoed the claim that "the Muslim world" was consumed by anger, and had long been so. The Associated Press offered a look back at "five other incidents that inspired rage in the Muslim world," crediting over a billion people for the actions of a few thousand in their search for historical continuity. Others took a psychoanalytic approach. "Why is the Muslim world so easily offended?" asked *Washington Post* columnist Fouad Ajami. "Madness in the Muslim World: Help Me Understand," pleaded a blogger for the *Houston Chronicle*.

It is time to retire the phrase "the Muslim world" from Western media. Using the phrase in the manner above disregards not only history and politics, but accurate reporting of contemporary events. The protests that took place around the world ranged in scale and intensity, in the participants' willingness to use violence, and in their rationales. The majority of "the Muslim world" did not participate in these protests, nor did all of the Muslims who protested the video advocate the bloodshed that took place in Libya.

By reducing a complex set of causes and conflicts to the rage of an amorphous mass, the Western media reinforce the very stereotype of a united, violent "Muslim world" that both the makers of the anti-Islam video and the Islamist instigators of the violence perpetuate.

Misleading Generalizations

Essentialist views of Islam and Muslims are nothing new. In Western media, Islam is often presented as a contagion, with Muslims as the afflicted, helpless to their own hostile impulses. What is different about the current crisis is that it comes in the aftermath of the "Arab Spring"— another series of intricate events depicted as interconnected and inevitable. Democracy would "spread" from one Muslim country to another, analysts argued, regardless of the unique historical trajectories of individual states. Some analysts went so far as to suggest it would spread to Central Asia, a region of largely isolationist dictatorships uninfluenced by Middle Eastern politics. The current protests are being portrayed as an "Arab Winter"—a simplistic reversal of a simplistic perception of success, with Muslims, undifferentiated, receiving the blame.

There is, of course, cohesion among Muslims, in the sense that there is cohesion among followers of any faith. The notion of the *umma* is an essential part of Islamic doctrine. But the way the idea of "the Muslim world" is expressed within Islamic communities is different from the way it is expressed outside them. It is rare to hear the phrase "the Christian world" used in the English-language media, because doing so would generalize about the motives of over 2 billion people. No such respect applies to the world's 1.5 billion Muslims. Googling the phrase "the Christian world" yields 5.8 million results, while the phrase "the Muslim world" gives over 87 million results, many of them wondering what is "wrong" with the queried target. When the phrase "the Muslim world" is invoked, it is usually to reduce, denigrate, or impugn.

The Western media's broad-stroke regionalism means that conflicts within individual Muslim-majority states become marginalized. Syrians posting on Twitter wondered how the world could give so much attention to a conflict that killed seven people while dozens of Syrians are killed by state security forces every day—documenting, as one commenter noted, their own demise in videos that receive far less attention than the bigoted pseudo-cinema of one American. Similarly, the violence at the diplomatic missions in Cairo and Benghazi was initially conflated, with "Muslim rage" being presented as a root cause for two distinct conflicts. The tendency to see "the Muslim world" as a problem in general means that specific problems within Muslim countries go unseen.

Dispelling Stereotypes

Soon after the destruction of the U.S. embassy in Benghazi and the deaths of four Americans, a protest was held against the men who murdered them. Libyan citizens held English-language signs declaring "Benghazi is against terrorism" and "Sorry Americans this is not the behavior of our Islam and Profit [sic]." Photos of the protest, distributed by Libya Alhurra Livestream, went viral on Facebook and Twitter.

The Libyans protesting were aware that not only Libyans, but Muslims in general, would be blamed for the violence that took place, because the small group of Muslims who stormed the embassy would be seen as representative of all. They gave the rare apology that Western commentators often encourage Muslims to make on behalf of others who commit violence in the name of Islam. But while the sentiment of the protestors is appreciated by many Americans—and the photos likely assuaged some prejudices—such explanations should not be necessary. Ordinary people should not be assumed to share the beliefs of violent criminals who share their faith.

Innocence of Muslims was made by Nakoula Basseley Nakoula, an Egyptian American who hates Muslims. It was found on YouTube and put on Egyptian television by news show host Sheikh Khaled Abdullah, a man trying to convince the world that Americans hate Muslims. This was a perfect storm of gross and deceitful parties depicting each other in the vilest terms, and then living up to each other's worst expectations.

The answer to such invective is not to reinforce it through media portrayals of "Muslims" as a collective. The media should instead pay more attention to individual states, conflicts, and leaders, since dictatorship and factionalism have been as essential in shaping politics in Muslim-majority regions as has religion. The current crisis demonstrates how corrupt parties use religion as an incitement to violence and a means to political gain. The Western media should not play party to their prejudices.

—*Originally published September 16, 2012*

In the Trial of Trayvon, the U.S. Is Guilty

When I was a child I watched policemen beat a man nearly to death, and I watched my country acquit them. I was shocked that police would attack a man instead of defending him. I was shocked that someone would record the attack on video and that this video would mean nothing. I was shocked that people could watch things and not really see them. I was shocked because I was a child. I was shocked because I am white.

Twenty-one years after the Rodney King verdict, Americans have proven again that in a court of law, perception matters more than proof. Perception is rooted in power, a power bestowed upon birth, reified through experience, and verified through discrimination masked as fairness and fact.

Trayvon Martin is dead and the man who killed him walks free. Americans are afraid there will be riots, like there were after the King verdict in 1992. But we should not fear riots. We should fear a society that puts people on trial the day they are born. And after they die.

Recession-fueled Racism

The Trayvon Martin trial was not supposed to happen. This is true in two respects. The Trayvon Martin trial only took place because public outrage prompted Florida police to arrest George Zimmerman, the man who killed him, over a month after Martin's death. The Trayvon Martin trial took place because that same public went on to try Martin in his own murder, assessing his morality like it precluded his right to live. It was never a trial of George Zimmerman. It was always a trial of Trayvon Martin, always a character assassination of the dead.

Over the past few decades, the U.S. has turned into a country where the circumstances into which you are born increasingly determine who you can become. Social mobility has stalled as wages stagnate and the cost of living soars. Exponential increases in university tuition have erased the possibility of education as a path out of poverty. These are not revelations—these are hard limitations faced by most Americans. But when confronted with systematic social and economic discrimination, even on a massive scale, the individual is often blamed. The poor, the unemployed, the lacking, are vilified for the things they lack.

One might assume that rising privation would increase public empathy toward minorities long denied a semblance of a fair shot. But instead, overt racism and racial barriers in

America have increased since the recession. Denied by the Supreme Court, invalidated in the eyes of many by the election of a black president, racism erases the individual until the individual is dead, where he is then recast as the enemy.

Trayvon Martin was vilified for being Trayvon Martin. If he were considered a fully human being, a person of inherent worth, it would be the U.S. on trial. For its denial of opportunity, for its ceaseless condemnation of the suffering, for its demonization of the people it abandons, for its shifting gaze from the burden of proof. The Trayvon Martin case only sanctioned what was once tacit and disavowed: A young black man can be murdered on perception. A young black man becomes the criminal so that the real criminal can go free.

Americans should not fear riots. They should fear a society that ranks the death of children based on their race. They should fear a society that shrugs, carries on, and lets them go.

A Tragedy

A friend of mine on Facebook posts updates from a website called "Black and Missing but Not Forgotten." The site exists because the default assumption is that a missing black child will be forgotten. It exists because the disappearance of a black child is considered less important than the disappearance of a white child. It exists because a large number of Americans have to be reminded that black children are human beings.

In June, the Supreme Court invalidated part of the Voting Rights Act, stating that "our country has changed," implying that discrimination against African Americans was a thing of the past. In May, the city of Chicago shut down public schools in which the majority of students were black. In April, a black high school student, Kiera Wilmot, was prosecuted as an adult after her science project exploded. In February, *The Onion* called nine-year-old black actress Quvenzhané Wallis an extremely vulgar name. The U.S., which proclaims racism a thing of the past, abandons and vilifies black children.

Many Americans of many races will be outraged that George Zimmerman has gone free. They will advocate for tolerance and peace. This is a noble sentiment, but what the U.S. needs is a cold, hard look at social structure. We need to examine and eliminate barriers to opportunity, some of which are racially biased in an overt way, but many of which are downplayed because they are considered ambiguous social issues—such as decaying public schools, low-wage labor, and unemployment, which affect African Americans at disproportionate rates.

Trayvon Martin was murdered before we could see what kind of person he would become. But the truth is, he had a hard road ahead of him no matter what he did. He would have confronted an America of racial and class barriers that even the most ambitious young man cannot override without a good deal of luck.

In a U.S. of diminished opportunities, luck is nothing to bank on. Neither is hope, or dreams, or the idea, espoused by President Obama, that for young black men, "there's no longer any room for excuses." Trayvon Martin shows that there is plenty of room for excuses. There is even more room for social and economic reform, for accountability, and for change.

Above all, there is room for responsibility. The death of Trayvon Martin is a U.S. tragedy. He was part of a broken system we all experience, but that black Americans experience in ways white Americans cannot fathom. The children who grow up like Trayvon Martin, discriminated against and denied opportunity, are everyone's responsibility. Providing them a fairer, safer future should be a public priority.

Americans should not fear riots. They should fear apathy. They should fear acquiescence. They should not fear each other. But it is understandable, now, that they do.

—*Originally published July 14, 2013*

St. Louis's Sons,
Taken Too Soon

There is a park near my house in St. Louis where I walk every day. To get there I walk past empty stores and vacant lots, past a brick whitewashed church onto which the proprietor painted decorative windows to make it look like the kind of place it could be if anyone around here had money.

The park is always busy. Families hold barbecues, children climb trees, young men shoot baskets, fathers coach sports. Almost everyone who goes to this park is black. When I walk through the park, white policemen ask me if anyone is bothering me. When I walk through the park, black men preface inquiries for directions with the phrase "Don't worry, I'm not going to hurt you."

Those are the assumptions that come from living in St. Louis. Sometimes they are spoken, but usually they are just felt.

At the far end of the park there is a teddy bear and a balloon tied to a tree. They were left there to commemorate a twenty-year-old man who was shot and killed in July. Makeshift memorials like this line the landscape of St. Louis. They remind passersby that the person who died was someone's son: not an archetype or a statistic or a threat, but a son.

Those the public are taught to fear are often the ones in danger.

The shooting happened near a high school reunion in late July. It had nothing to do with the reunion, an annual park affair attended by enthusiastic graduates of a 90 percent–black public school system. The shooting, which took place in another part of the park, seems to have been the violent outcome of a private feud.

But around St. Louis, on the Internet, the chatter began. On websites, white St. Louisans speculated on the inherent danger of such a large gathering of black citizens. They stated again and again that they were not surprised.

A shooting in St. Louis is never surprising, but it will always be shocking: that the cruelty of the act is complemented by the callousness of the reaction; that when a community cries, someone always finds a way to give it more to grieve.

Decades of Violence

When Michael Brown was shot, many of us in St. Louis heard about it on the Internet before we saw it in the news. I saw it on the Instagram account of Tef Poe, a rapper and writer who has emerged as one of St. Louis's many black activist leaders. He posted a picture of a man, Brown's stepfather, holding a cardboard sign that read: "Ferguson police just executed my unarmed son."

It took hours for the media to report on the story. Initial reports from the local paper referred to the gathering of a crowd outside where Brown's body laid in the street for four hours as a "mob reaction." They retracted that description as momentum grew, as a casualty so horrifyingly common became recognized as the crisis it was.

If you had asked whether the killing of Brown would become an international cause or be swept silently aside, most would have bet on the latter. It is a testament to black St. Louis activists, and their ceaseless documentation and calls to action, that it was not.

No one will forget the killing of Michael Brown. But that killing was preceded by decades of police brutality, of violence, of losses, of teddy bears tied to trees. During the 2013–14 school year, seventeen St. Louis public school children died, a record number. The second largest number, in 2010, was eight.

"At some schools, kids don't come back to school for several days when a young person has died in the kind of violent death that occurred last night because they think there may be repercussions," a St. Louis school superintendent told local media in March, after an eleven-year-old black boy was shot through the window of his home.

By spring, trauma counselors were working overtime. Now, after the death of Brown and the tear-gassing of the local population, including children, they work around the clock.

St. Louis was grieving long before the tragedy of Ferguson—or, at least, parts of it were. Like everything else in St. Louis, grief is unequally allocated. This is a city where people live their whole lives seeing certain neighborhoods only on TV.

St. Louis is a city where black communities are watched—by police, by spectators—more than they are seen, more than they are heard.

Healing St. Louis

At my daughter's bus stop in St. Louis, the children would play games. They would chase each other and run, laughing and screaming, through neighbors' yards. "You better watch it," one child called to another. "I'm going to call the police. And it doesn't matter what you do. They'll put you in jail for nothing."

A white classmate asked the boy, who was black, what he meant. He said that had happened to his uncle. The white boy looked at the black boy blankly. You can live next to your neighbor and still exist in a different city, with different rights and rules. You can greet each other with sincere warmth, and never fathom the disparity of experience.

In January, my daughter's school held an event to celebrate the life of Dr. Martin Luther King Jr. They called it "MLK: Not a Day, but a Way." We marched through the neighborhood, parents and children and local leaders, to show that the struggle against injustice was never over. But we all marched to different beats, to different histories, and it would have been foolish to pretend otherwise.

In the auditorium, in a great public school that is, like so many primarily black St. Louis public schools, in danger of losing accreditation, we sang "We Shall Overcome." My daughter clasped hands with a black boy, her partner in the after-school science club. They sang a few bars then lost the words, and began whispering to each other about the movie *Frozen*.

It was a scene of childhood innocence that advocates of a post-racial society like to promote: a black boy and a white girl, sweetly holding hands. But like all childhood innocence, it is an illusion. That boy will find danger when he ventures into the world unless St. Louis—and all U.S. cities—changes its ways.

There is a movement to heal St. Louis. For St. Louis to heal, we need to examine the deep wounds inflicted by decades of discrimination and distrust. We need to protect the young black men who are threatened but portrayed as threats. Michael Brown is one of St. Louis's many sons taken too soon.

—*Originally published August 27, 2014*

The Freedom to Criticize
Free Speech

I n the summer of 2012, thousands of people took to the streets to protest a perceived assault on their religion. Traditional values were under attack, the protestors claimed, thanks to the meddling antics of Westerners seeking to disparage conservative views. But in this deeply divided and staunchly sectarian part of the world, it was not long before a counterprotest emerged. Activists picketed the sites of the original demonstrations, condemning the first group's actions as backward and inhumane. Media pundits from both sides spurred on the controversy, which dragged on for weeks, while politicians exploited it to their own advantage. Meanwhile, people from outside the region looked on in disdain. How could so much outrage be generated over something so trivial?

I am talking, of course, about Chick-fil-A.

Those wondering how the low-grade YouTube clip *Innocence of Muslims* managed to incite revolt would do well to remember that America spent the summer of 2012 having religiously motivated protests over a chicken sandwich. On June 16, Dan Cathy, the CEO of the fast food restaurant Chick-fil-A, announced that he opposed same-sex marriage on biblical grounds, saying that gay rights advocates were "inviting God's judgment on our nation." Cathy had donated millions in proceeds from Chick-fil-A to anti-gay activist groups, including groups who want to make "gay behavior" illegal.

In July, gay rights advocates called for a boycott of the fast food chain, companies cut contracts for corporate tie-ins, and politicians contemplated a ban of the restaurant in several cities, with one mayor accusing Cathy of peddling "hate chicken." Americans who shared Cathy's views were outraged. On August 1, over 630,000 people showed up for "Chick-fil-A Appreciation Day," an event organized by conservative Christian politician Mike Huckabee to celebrate the restaurant's willingness "to take a stand for the Godly values we espouse." Two days later, gay rights activists held a "Chick-fil-A Kiss Day," in which same-sex couples were encouraged to show affection at the chicken chains.

Advocates of the Chick-fil-A boycott saw it as a matter of civil rights. They were not comfortable giving their money to an organization that donated it to groups that promoted discrimination. Those who opposed the boycott were largely conservative Christians who shared Cathy's view that same-sex marriage is wrong. But that was not how they framed their argument. Instead, they presented it as a matter of freedom of speech.

The Fine Lines of Speech

According to the Chick-fil-A supporters, Dan Cathy's constitutional rights had been violated. "Calling for the boycott . . . has a chilling effect on our 1st Amendment rights," said Sarah Palin, adding that Cathy was getting "crucified" for "having voiced support for kind of that [sic] cornerstone of all civilization and all religions since the beginning of time." One Virginia demonstrator, who admitted that she opposed same-sex marriage, said that the protest was "more about people frankly being offended that people are offended."

The United States has been said to have an exceptional free speech environment. From a legal perspective, that is true: racial insults, flag burning, and desecration of religious materials are all permitted by law. In practice, attitudes toward free speech are more diverse and complicated. The line between advocating for free speech and seeming to applaud what people say is often blurred, as is the line between censorship and condemnation.

Chick-fil-A defenders like Palin believe that to call for a boycott against an organization that promotes hateful speech is to threaten freedom of speech as a whole. But while the politicians who argued against allowing Chick-fil-A in their cities may have overreacted, the protest was aimed at getting people to avoid an organization that encouraged intolerance. It was not aimed at preventing Cathy or others from expressing their intolerant views.

To condemn hateful speech, or call for a protest against those who promote it, is itself a form of free speech. Announcing that you are offended when someone insults you or something you believe in is not an act of censorship. What person would refrain from issuing a rejoinder against those who insult him on the grounds that the right to insult precludes the right to defend? It is worth remembering this in light of *Innocence of Muslims* and the hostile rhetoric against those whom it offends.

Shock and Offense

On September 19, the French magazine *Charlie Hebdo* published cartoons ridiculing the Prophet Muhammad, including several in which he is depicted in lewd positions. Their justification: freedom of speech. "Freedom of the press, is that a provocation?" the editor of the magazine asked, adding that the images will "shock those who will want to be shocked." The French government banned people from protesting the cartoons. They said they were protecting freedom of speech while denying citizens the right to demonstrate their disapproval.

Shock and offense are not feelings people cultivate. They are spontaneous emotions that reflect a violation of a person's sense of self. When someone is shocked or offended, it is natural that they would express it. Yet when Muslims offended by *Innocence of Muslims* or *Charlie Hebdo*'s cartoons do so, they are accused of being an enemy of free speech. There is no excuse for reacting to an insult with violence. But many Muslims who peacefully expressed their condemnation of views that are hateful to them have been lumped into the same category: "Why are Muslims so easily offended?" goes the refrain.

Worse yet, the creators of the cartoons have been portrayed as heroes for mocking Islam in a country known for its hostility toward Muslim immigrants and fierce state protection of free speech provocateurs. Editorials around the world have lauded the magazine for its alleged bravery, with one author proclaiming, "If free speech means anything, it's the right to say and publish things that other people find objectionable and irresponsible, even blasphemous."

Such a perspective confuses what free speech does with what free speech means. Free speech allows people to insult and berate each other, but that is not what most people want, and it is rarely what makes freedom of speech attractive to those who do not have it. Those forced to live in countries without free speech know that one of its greatest values is that it allows citizens to speak the truth about their position, to contest false depictions, to refute bias and slander.

Free speech means not only the right to offend, but the right to defend. When Dan Cathy proclaims his prejudice against homosexuals, or *Charlie Hebdo* its hatred of Muslims, that is free speech. But when gay rights groups call for a boycott, and Muslims protest a cartoon or a movie, that is also free speech. Free speech does not mean deferring to people's right to abuse you.

The Ingredients of Free Speech

In America, a nation was divided by a sandwich. Across the world, people are dying because of a Z-grade film trailer. The battle lines of free speech are often drawn over the banal. One strategy of those who seek to minimize the argument of the offended party is to scoff at what inspired it. It's only a restaurant, only a movie, only a cartoon—why the outrage? they ask.

But such conflicts are rarely about the object in question. They are about the participants and their culture, their ideologies and their faith. They are about sanction and censure, about whose dignity can withstand whose degradation.

Freedom of speech is protected by law but guided by emotion. We should not mistake legal sanction for personal approval, but we should also not mistake personal disapproval for a rejection of free speech. In free societies, people have the right to say hateful things. And those offended have the right to oppose and condemn them.

—Originally published September 25, 2012

PART IV

Higher Education

The Closing of American
Academia

t is 2011 and I'm sitting in the Palais des Congres in Montreal, watching anthropologists talk about structural inequality.

The American Anthropological Association meeting is held annually to showcase research from around the world, and like thousands of other anthropologists, I am paying to play: $650 for airfare, $400 for three nights in a "student" hotel, $70 for membership, and $94 for admission. The latter two fees are student rates. If I were an unemployed or underemployed scholar, the rates would double.

The theme of this year's meeting is "Traces, Tidemarks and Legacies." According to the explanation on the American Anthropological Association website, we live in a time when "the meaning and location of differences, both intellectually and morally, have been rearranged." As the conference progresses, I begin to see what they mean. I am listening to the speaker bemoan the exploitative practices of the neo-liberal model when a friend of mine taps me on the shoulder.

"I spent almost my entire salary to be here," she says.

My friend is an adjunct. She has a PhD in anthropology and teaches at a university where she is paid $2,100 per course. While she is a professor, she is not a Professor. She is, like 67 percent of American university faculty, a part-time employee on a contract that may or may not be renewed each semester. She receives no benefits or health care.

According to the Adjunct Project, a crowdsourced website revealing adjunct wages—data that universities have long kept under wraps—her salary is about average. If she taught five classes a year, a typical full-time faculty course load, she would make $10,500, well below the poverty line. Some ad-juncts make more. I have one friend who was offered $5,000 per course, but he turned it down and requested less so that his children would still qualify for food stamps.

Why is my friend, a smart woman with no money, spending nearly $2,000 to attend a conference she cannot afford? She is looking for a way out. In America, academic hiring is rigid and seasonal. Each discipline has a confer-ence, usually held in the fall, where interviews take place. These interviews can be announced only days or even hours in advance, so most people book a conference beforehand, often to receive no interviews at all.

The American Anthropological Association tends to hold its meetings in America's most expensive cities, although they do have one stipulation: "AAA staff responsible for negotiating and administering annual meeting contracts shall show preference to locales with living wage ordinances." This rule does not apply, unfortunately, to those in attendance.

Below the Poverty Line

In most professions, salaries below the poverty line would be cause for alarm. In academia, they are treated as a source of gratitude. Volunteerism is par for the course—literally. Teaching is touted as a "calling," with compensation an afterthought. One American research university offers its PhD students a salary of $1,000 per semester for the "opportunity" to design and teach a course for undergraduates, who are each paying about $50,000 in tuition. The university calls this position "senior teaching assistant" because paying an instructor so far below minimum wage is probably illegal.

> I struggle with the limited opportunities in academia for Americans like me, people for whom education was once a path out of poverty, and not a way into it.

In addition to teaching, academics conduct research and publish, but they are not paid for this work either. Instead, all proceeds go to for-profit academic publishers, who block academic articles from the public through exorbitant download and subscription fees, making millions for themselves in the process. If authors want to make their research public, they have to pay the publisher an average of $3,000 per article. Without an institutional affiliation, an academic cannot access scholarly research without paying, even for articles written by the scholar herself.

It may be hard to summon sympathy for people who walk willingly into such working conditions. "Bart, don't make fun of grad students," Marge told her son on an oft-quoted episode of *The Simpsons*. "They just made a terrible life choice."

But all Americans should be concerned about adjuncts, and not only because adjuncts are the ones teaching our youth. The adjunct problem is emblematic of broader trends in American employment: the end of higher education as a means to prosperity, and the severing of opportunity to all but the most privileged.

In a searing commentary, political analyst Joshua Foust notes that the unpaid internships, which were once limited to show business, have now spread to nearly every industry. "It's almost impossible to get a job working on policy in this town without an unpaid internship," he writes from Washington, D.C., one of the most expensive cities in the country. Even law, once a safety net for American strivers, is now a profession which pays as little as $10,000 a year—unfeasible for all but the wealthy, and devastating for those who have invested more than $100,000 into their degrees. One after another, the occupations that shape American society are becoming impossible for all but the most elite to enter.

The Value of a Degree

Academia is vaunted for being a meritocracy. Publications are judged on blind review, and good graduate programs offer free tuition and a decent stipend. But academia's reliance on adjuncts makes it no different than fields that cater to the elite through unpaid internships.

Anthropologists are known for their attentiveness to social inequality, but few have acknowledged the plight of their peers. When I expressed doubt about the job market to one colleague, she advised me, with total seriousness, to "reevaluate what work means" and to consider "post-work imaginaries." A popular video on post-graduate employment cuts to the chase: "Why don't you tap into your trust fund?"

In May 2012, I received my PhD, but I still do not know what to do with it. I struggle with the closed-off nature of academic work, which I think should be accessible to everyone, but most of all I struggle with the limited opportunities in academia for Americans like me, people for whom education was once a path out of poverty, and not a way into it.

My father, the first person in his family to go to college, tries to tell me my degree has value. "Our family came here with nothing," he says of my great-grandparents, who fled Poland a century ago. "Do you know how incredible it is that you did this, how proud they would be?"

And my heart broke a little when he said that, because his illusion is so touching—so revealing of the values of his generation, and so alien to the experience of mine.

—Originally published August 20, 2012

Academic Paywalls Mean
Publish and Perish

On July 19, 2011, Aaron Swartz, a computer programmer and activist, was arrested for downloading 4.8 million academic articles. The articles constituted nearly the entire catalog of JSTOR, a scholarly research database. Universities that want to use JSTOR are charged as much as $50,000 in annual subscription fees.

Individuals who want to use JSTOR must shell out an average of $19 per article. The academics who write the articles are not paid for their work, nor are the academics who review it. The only people who profit are the 211 employees of JSTOR.

Swartz thought this was wrong. The paywall, he argued, constituted "private theft of public culture." It hurt not only the greater public but also academics, who must "pay money to read the work of their colleagues."

For attempting to make scholarship accessible to people

who cannot afford it, Swartz is facing a $1 million fine and up to thirty-five years in prison. The severity of the charges shocked activists fighting for open-access publication. But it shocked academics too, for different reasons.

"Can you imagine if JSTOR was public?" one of my friends in academia wondered. "That means someone might actually read my article."

Academic publishing is structured on exclusivity. Originally, this exclusivity had to do with competition within journals. Acceptance rates at top journals are low, in some disciplines under 5 percent, and publishing in prestigious venues was once an indication of one's value as a scholar.

Today, publishing in an academic journal all but ensures that your writing will go unread. "The more difficult it is to get an article into a journal, the higher the perceived value of having done so," notes Kathleen Fitzpatrick, the director of Scholarly Communication at the Modern Language Association. "But this sense of prestige too easily shades over into a sense that the more exclusively a publication is distributed, the higher its value."

Discussions of open-access publishing have centered on whether research should be made free to the public. But this question sets up a false dichotomy between "the public" and "the scholar." Many people fall into a gray zone, the boundaries of which are determined by institutional affiliation and personal wealth. This gray category includes independent scholars, journalists, public officials, writers, scientists, and others who are experts in their fields yet are unwilling or unable to pay for access to academic research.

This denial of resources is a loss to those who value scholarly inquiry. But it is also a loss for the academics themselves, whose ability to stay employed rests on their willingness to limit the circulation of knowledge. In academia, the ability to prohibit scholarship is considered more meaningful than the ability to produce it.

"Publish and Perish"

When do scholars become part of "the public"? One answer may be when they cannot afford to access their own work. If I wanted to download my articles, I would have to pay $183. That is the total cost of the six academic articles I published between 2006 and 2012, the most expensive of which goes for 32£, or $51, and the cheapest of which is sold for $12, albeit with a mere 24 hours of access to it.

Since I receive no money from the sale of my work, I have no idea whether anyone purchased it. I suspect not, as the reason for the high price has nothing to do with making money. JSTOR, for example, makes only 0.35 percent of its profits from individual article sales. The high price is designed to maintain the barrier between academia and the outside world. Paywalls codify and commodify tacit elitism.

In academia, publishing is a strategic enterprise. It is less about the production of knowledge than where that knowledge will be held (or withheld) and what effect that has on the author's career. New professors are awarded tenure based on their publication output, but not on the impact of their research on the world—perhaps because, due to paywalls, it is usually minimal.

"Publish or perish" has long been an academic maxim. In the digital economy, "publish and perish" may be a more apt summation. What academics gain in professional security, they lose in public relevance, a sad fate for those who want their research appreciated and understood.

Many scholars hate this situation. Over the last decade, there has been a push to end paywalls and move toward a more inclusive model. But advocates of open access face an uphill battle even as the segregation of scholarship leads to the loss of financial support.

In the United States, granting agencies like the National Science Foundation have come under attack by politicians who believe they fund projects irrelevant to public life. But by denying the public access to their work, academics do not allow taxpayers to see where their money is spent. By refusing to engage a broader audience about their research, academics ensure that few will defend them when funding for that research is cut.

Tyranny of Academic Publishers

One of the saddest moments I had in graduate school was when a professor advised me on when to publish. "You have to space out your articles by when it will benefit you professionally," he said, when I told him I wanted to get my research out as soon as possible. "Don't use up all your ideas before you're on the tenure track." This confused me.

Was I supposed to have a finite number of ideas? Was it my professional obligation to withhold them?

What I did not understand is that academic publishing is not about sharing ideas. It is about removing oneself from public scrutiny while scrambling for professional security. It is about making work "count" with the few while sequestering it from the many.

Soon after the arrest of Aaron Swartz, a technologist named Gregory Maxwell dumped over eighteen thousand JSTOR documents on the torrent website The Pirate Bay. "All too often journals, galleries and museums are becoming not disseminators of knowledge—as their lofty mission statements suggest—but censors of knowledge, because censoring is the one thing they do better than the Internet does," he wrote.

He described how he had wanted to republish the original scientific writings of astronomer William Herschel where people reading the Wikipedia entry for Uranus could find them. In the current publishing system, this constitutes a criminal act.

Maxwell and Swartz were after a simple thing: for the public to engage with knowledge. This is supposed to be what academics are after, too. Many of them are, but they are not able to pursue that goal due to the tyranny of academic publishers and professional norms that encourage obsequiousness and exclusion.

The academic publishing industry seems poised to collapse before it changes. But some scholars are writing about the current crisis. Last month, an article called "Public

Intellectuals, Online Media and Public Spheres: Current Realignments" was published in the *International Journal of Politics, Culture and Society*.

I would tell you what it says, but I do not know. It is behind a paywall.

—*Originally published October 2, 2012*
Note: Aaron Swartz unfortunately
committed suicide in January 2013.

Academia's Indentured Servants

On April 8, 2013, *The New York Times* reported that 76 percent of American university faculty are adjunct professors—an all-time high. Unlike tenured faculty, whose annual salaries can top $160,000, adjunct professors make an average of $2,700 per course and receive no health care or other benefits.

Most adjuncts teach at multiple universities while still not making enough to stay above the poverty line. Some are on welfare or homeless. Others depend on charity drives held by their peers. Adjuncts are generally not allowed to have offices or participate in faculty meetings. When they ask for a living wage or benefits, they can be fired. Their contingent status allows them no recourse.

No one forces a scholar to work as an adjunct. So why do some of America's brightest PhDs—many of whom are authors of books and articles on labor, power, or injustice—accept such terrible conditions?

"Path dependence and sunk costs must be powerful forces," speculates political scientist Steve Saideman in a blog post titled "Adjuncting Mystery." In other words, job candidates have invested so much time and money into their professional training that they cannot fathom abandoning their goal—even if this means living, as Saideman says, like "second-class citizens." (He later downgraded this to "third-class citizens.")

With roughly 40 percent of academic positions eliminated since the 2008 crash, most adjuncts will not find a tenure-track job. Their path dependence and sunk costs will likely lead to greater path dependence and sunk costs—and the costs of the academic job market are prohibitive. Many job candidates must shell out thousands of dollars for a chance to interview at their discipline's annual meeting, usually held in one of the most expensive cities in the world. In some fields, candidates must pay to even see the job listings.

Given the need for personal wealth as a means to entry, one would assume that adjuncts would be even more outraged about their plight. After all, their paltry salaries and lack of departmental funding make their job hunt a far greater sacrifice than for those with means. But this is not the case. While efforts at labor organization are emerging, the adjunct rate continues to soar—from 68 percent in 2008, the year of the economic crash, to 76 percent just five years later.

Contingency has become permanent, a rite of passage to nowhere.

A Twofold Crisis

The adjunct plight is indicative of a twofold crisis in education and in the American economy. On one hand, we have the degradation of education in general and higher education in particular. It is no surprise that when 76 percent of professors are viewed as so disposable and indistinguishable that they are listed in course catalogs as "Professor Staff," administrators view computers that grade essays as a viable replacement. Those who promote inhumane treatment tend not to favor the human.

On the other hand, we have a pervasive self-degradation among low-earning academics—a sweeping sense of shame that strikes adjunct workers before adjunct workers can strike. In a tirade for *Slate* subtitled "Getting a literature Ph.D. will turn you into an emotional trainwreck, not a professor," Rebecca Schuman writes: "By the time you finish—if you even do—your academic self will be the culmination of your entire self, and thus you will believe, incomprehensibly, that not having a tenure-track job makes you worthless. You will believe this so strongly that when you do not land a job, it will destroy you."

Self-degradation sustains the adjunct economy, and we see echoes of it in journalism, policy, and other fields in which unpaid or underpaid labor is increasingly the norm.

It is easy to make people work for less than they are worth when they are conditioned to feel worthless.

In his 2004 article in *The Chronicle of Higher Education*, "Is Graduate School a Cult?" Thomas H. Benton wrote:

> "Although I am currently a tenure-track professor of English, I realize that nothing but luck distinguishes me from thousands of other highly-qualified Ph.D.'s in the humanities who will never have full-time academic jobs and, as a result, are symbolically dead to the academy."

Benton's answer to his own question is yes, and he offers a list of behavior controls used by cults—"no critical questions about leader, doctrine, or policy seen as legitimate," "access to non-cult sources of information minimized or discouraged"—that mirror the practices of graduate school. The author lived as he wrote: it was later revealed that "Thomas H. Benton" was a pseudonym used by academic William Pannapacker for *The Chronicle of Higher Education* piece—a publication said to employ more pseudonyms than any other American newspaper. The life of the mind is born of fear.

Some may wonder why adjuncts do not get a well-paying non-academic job while they search for a tenure-track position. The answer lies in the cult-like practices Pannapacker describes. To work outside of academia, even temporarily, signals you are not "serious" or "dedicated" to scholarship. It does not matter if you are simply too poor to stay: in academia, perseverance is redefined as the ability to suffer silently or to survive on family wealth. As a result, scholars serve as adjuncts in order to retain an institutional affiliation, while the institution offers them no respect in return.

Dispensable Automatons

Is academia a cult? That is debatable, but it is certainly a caste system. Outspoken academics like Pannapacker are rare: most tenured faculty have stayed silent about the adjunct crisis. "It is difficult to get a man to understand something when his job depends on not understanding it," wrote Upton Sinclair, the American author famous for his essays on labor exploitation. Somewhere in America, a tenured professor may be teaching about his work as a nearby adjunct holds office hours out of her car.

On Twitter, I asked why so many professors who study injustice ignore the plight of their peers. "They don't consider us their peers," the adjuncts wrote back. Academia likes to think of itself as a meritocracy—which it is not—and those who have tenured jobs like to think they deserved them. They probably do—but with hundreds of applications per available position, an awful lot of deserving candidates have defaulted to the adjunct track.

The plight of the adjunct shows how personal success is not an excuse to dismiss systemic failure. Success is meaningless when the system that sustained it—the higher education system—is no longer sustainable. When it falls, everyone falls. Success is not a pathway out of social responsibility.

Last week, a corporation proudly announced that it had created a digital textbook that monitors whether students had done the reading. This followed the announcement of the software that grades essays, which followed months of hype over MOOCs—massive online open courses—replacing classroom interaction. Professors who can gauge student engagement through class discussion are unneeded. Professors who can offer thoughtful feedback on student writing are unneeded. Professors who interact with students, who care about students, are unneeded.

We should not be surprised that it has come to this when 76 percent of faculty are treated as dispensable automatons. The contempt for adjuncts reflects a general contempt for learning. The promotion of information has replaced the pursuit of knowledge. But it is not enough to have information—we need insight and understanding, and above all, we need people who can communicate it to others.

People who have the ability to do this are not dispensable. They should not see themselves this way, and they should not be treated this way. Fight for what you are worth, adjuncts. Success is solidarity.

—*Originally published April 11, 2013*

The Political Consequences of Academic Paywalls

The suicide of Aaron Swartz, the activist committed to making scholarly research accessible to everyone, has renewed debate about the ethics of academic publishing. Under the current system, academic research is housed in scholarly databases that charge as much as $50 per article to those without a university affiliation.

The only people who profit from this system are academic publishers. Scholars receive no money from the sale of their articles, and are marginalized by a public who cannot afford to read their work. Ordinary people are denied access to information and prohibited from engaging in scholarly debate.

Academic paywalls are often presented as a moral or financial issue. How can one justify profiting off unpaid labor while denying the public access to research frequently funded through taxpayer dollars? But paywalls also have broader political consequences. Whether or not an article is accessible affects more than just the author or reader. It affects anyone who could potentially benefit from scholarly insight, information, or expertise—that is, everyone.

The impact of the paywall is most significant in places where censorship and propaganda reign. When information is power, the paywall privileges the powerful. Dictatorships are the paywall's unwitting beneficiary.

Publishing as a Means to Freedom

In 2006, I wrote an article proving that the government of Uzbekistan had fabricated a terrorist group in order to justify shooting hundreds of Uzbek civilians gathered at a protest in the city of Andijon. Like all peer-reviewed academic articles, "Inventing Akromiya: The Role of Uzbek Propagandists in the Andijon Massacre" was published in a journal and sequestered from public view. In 2008, I published the article on academia.edu, a website where scholars can upload their works as pdfs on individual home pages. This had consequences beyond what I had anticipated.

At the time my article was published, hundreds of Uzbeks had fled across the border to Kyrgyzstan, from where they were relocated as refugees to Western states. Among these Uzbeks were witnesses to the shooting in Andijon as well as people who were accused of being members of Akromiya—a loose collective of devout Muslim businessmen who were known for their financial acumen, charitable initiatives, and profound piety, all of which the government of Uzbekistan found threatening. The men of Akromiya—an appellative coined by an Uzbek propagandist after alleged leader Akrom Yo'ldoshev—bore no resemblance to the violent Islamic extremists depicted in Uzbek state literature.

Over the next few years, many Uzbeks linked to the Akromiya controversy began petitioning for political asylum. Because they had been labeled Islamic terrorists by the Uzbek government, they faced an uphill battle in the Western legal system. My academic article became a piece of evidence in many of these asylum cases, including one from the United Nations Refugee Agency, which cites the copy available at academia.edu. Because I made my work open, it helped keep innocent people from being deported to a country where they would be jailed or killed.

"Shielded from the People Who Need It Most"

When we talk about academic research being shielded from the general public, we forget that the general public includes non-academic experts to whom such research is directly relevant—such as lawyers, doctors, journalists, policy officials, and activists. Academics love to complain about superficial reporting or uninformed policy, but their own system denies professionals the opportunity to add depth to their work. With database subscription fees running to tens of thousands of dollars, even prestigious organizations cannot afford to penetrate the paywall.

I regularly receive requests for my academic articles,

and I always comply—as do most of the academics I know. Contrary to popular perception, most scholars want their work to be read. But for every researcher plaintively tweeting that they need a paywalled pdf, there are many for whom tracking down barricaded knowledge seems too much trouble. Instead, they rely on what resources are available. This means that a lot of academic research, some of which could have profound political implications, is ignored.

After the suicide of Aaron Swartz, many academics published their papers online and linked them on Twitter under the hashtag #pdftribute. They did this to honor Swartz's fight to make information available to more than the academic elite. Critics have argued that this action is essentially meaningless, as it fails to address the career incentive of the professoriate, whose ability to advance professionally rests on their willingness to publish in journals inaccessible to the public.

This is a valid point—for Western academics. For the rest of the world, it is irrelevant. When an activist needs information about the political conditions of her country, she should be able to read it. When a lawyer needs ammunition against a corrupt regime, she should be able to find it. When a journalist is struggling to cover a foreign conflict, she should have access to research on that country.

The specialization that makes academic work seem obscure or boring to a general audience is also what makes it uniquely valuable.

One could argue that non-academics sources suffice,

but that is not necessarily the case. The specialization that makes academic work seem obscure or boring to a general audience is also what makes it uniquely valuable. Academics cover topics in depth that few cover at all. Unfortunately, their expertise is shielded from the people who need it most.

Academic's Incentives Verus Society's Needs

Shortly after #pdftribute launched, a friend asked me whether she should post her articles online. She is an assistant professor who studies an authoritarian state. She has published a number of articles in paywalled scholarly journals. For this, she will probably get tenure.

My friend spends her free time educating the world about the conditions of this country through social media. She does not hoard her data. Instead she does everything possible to make it available to anyone who needs it. This ultimately included joining #pdftribute and publishing her articles online. For this, she could potentially get in trouble.

My friend knew she had to do what was right. As a scholar of an authoritarian regime, she understands that one of the greatest weapons of dictatorships is their ability to control information. She has witnessed firsthand the importance of accurate statistics, of open sources, of censored stories told. She knows what happens when those resources are denied.

Information is power, but information is also freedom. With that freedom comes responsibility. Scholars can no longer question whether their work is relevant to a broader audience, because in the digital age, that audience is simply too broad. All scholarly work is relevant to someone—and the impact can be profound. Whether we allow that impact to be realized remains to be seen.

—Originally published January 18, 2013

The Immorality of College Admissions

On October 6, *New York* magazine published an article on the demise of "ethical parenting." A new generation of parents were encouraging cheating, doing their children's homework, bribing powerful officials, and sabotaging their children's rivals.

"Parenthood means you cannot possibly behave as though society's rules and norms apply equally to all," writes the author of the article, Lisa Miller. She describes a social order in which the ends are believed to justify the means, regardless of who gets hurt. Miller attributes the rise of unethical parenting to a declining economy: "The accoutrements of middle-class stability and comfort feel like they're slipping away, even to those of us living smack in the middle of them."

What Miller never explicitly says is that every act of

lying, cheating, and cruelty she describes is directed at one goal: getting a child into a prestigious college. Nothing else drives the immoral behavior depicted, making one wonder—is it the parents who are unethical? Or is it higher education itself?

Miller's article is one of many trend pieces showcasing how parents sacrifice both their integrity and their bank accounts in the quest for college admission. *The New York Times* alone has run dozens of articles on high schools that cost $40,000 per year, preschools that cost $43,000 per year, and SAT tutors who charge $35,000 per student.

The luxurious world depicted in these articles is unfamiliar to the average American family, which makes $52,000 per year. One might wonder why the struggles of wealthy parents are covered so closely when they represent such a tiny percent of the population. That is, until you look at who comprises the entering classes of America's "need-blind" universities.

Faux Diversity

"Diversity" is a cherished value of American schools—so long as that diversity does not include students whose families earn less than the tuition fee. Elite universities favor those willing to pay to play—and play again until they win.

Only 3.8 percent of American families make more than $200,000 per year. But at Harvard University, 45.6 percent of incoming freshmen come from families making $200,000 or more. A mere 4 percent of Harvard students come from a family in the bottom quintile of U.S. incomes, and only 17.8 percent come from the bottom three quintiles.

"We admit students without any regard for financial need—a policy we call 'need-blind admission,'" Harvard's website proudly proclaims. Harvard charges $54,496 per year for tuition, and room and board, but waives the fees for families making less than $60,000 per year.

This would be a laudable policy were Harvard admitting low-income students in any significant numbers, but they are not. Instead, they fill their ranks with the children of the elite portrayed in Miller's article—elites who drop hundreds of thousands of dollars on private schools, exorbitant "enrichment" activities, and personal tutors that almost no American can afford.

Harvard's admission is "need-blind" only in that it turns a blind eye to actual need. Like many universities, it increases its number of aid recipients by inflating its price tag. With its tuition higher than the median U.S. household income, students from families making $200,000 are now deemed poor enough to qualify for financial aid.

"You can afford Harvard," the admissions site boasts, noting that 70 percent of students receive assistance. They neglect to mention that this 70 percent represents some of the wealthiest people in the country.

This is not to say that a family making $100,000 or even $200,000 does not merit financial aid to attend Harvard. They do, but only because Harvard charges obscenely high tuition, despite having an endowment of over $30 billion.

Their price tag functions as a social signifier and a "go away" sign, a sticker designed to shock—and deter.

Harvard is but one of many U.S. universities whose admissions policies ensure that the entering class is comprised of the ruling class. Studies by the New America Foundation note that most merit aid goes to wealthy families, and that "merit aid policy is associated with a decrease in the percentage of low-income and black students, particularly at the more selective institutions."

While universities like Harvard keep out the poor by redefining wealth as poverty, others practice more blatant discrimination. At George Washington University, students who cannot pay full tuition are put on a wait list while wealthier students are let in. In 2012, less than 1 percent of wait-listed students were admitted.

> *What they are defending is a system in which wealth is passed off as merit, in which credentials are not earned but bought.*

Like Harvard, George Washington had advertised itself as "need-blind" until revelations of its admissions process came to light. It now defines itself as "need aware"—a phrase which implies they are aware of need, but seemingly unconcerned with fulfilling it.

Wealth as Merit

Defenders of elite universities argue that the poor are not a target of discrimination, but are simply less qualified for admission. They point to lower SAT scores, a dearth of extracurricular activities, and lackluster standards of achievement at impoverished public schools.

What they are defending is a system in which wealth is passed off as merit, in which credentials are not earned but bought. Aptitude is a quality measured by how much money you can spend on its continual reassessment.

Students whose parents pay tens of thousands for SAT tutors to help their child take the test over and over compete against students who struggle to pay the fee to take the test once. Students who spend afternoons on "enrichment" activities compete against students working service jobs to pay bills—jobs which don't "count" in the admissions process. Students who shell out for exotic volunteer trips abroad compete with students of what C. Z. Nnaemeka termed "the un-exotic underclass"—the poor who have "the misfortune of being insufficiently interesting," the poor who make up most of the U.S. today.

For upper-class parents, the college admissions process has become a test of loyalty: What will you spend, what values will you compromise, for your child to be accepted? For lower-class parents, admissions is a test failed at birth: an absence of wealth disguised as a deficiency of merit. In the middle are the students, stranded players in a rigged game.

It does not have to be this way. Imagine a college application system in which applicants could only take standardized tests once. Imagine a system in which young people working jobs to support their families were valued as much as those who travel and "volunteer" on their parents' dime.

Imagine a system in which we value what a person does with what he has, instead of mistaking a lack of resources for a lack of ability.

Imagine a system in which a child's future does not rest on his parents' past.

A higher-education system that once promoted social mobility now serves to solidify class barriers. Desperate parents compromise their principles in order to spare their children rejection. But it is the system itself that must be rejected. True merit cannot be bought—and admission should not be either.

—Originally published October 29, 2013

College Is a Promise the
Economy Does Not Keep

n 2000, *New York Times* columnist David Brooks published
a sociological study of the United States that now reads
like science fiction. *Bobos in Paradise* chronicled how a
new upper class of "Bobos"—bourgeois bohemians—struggled to navigate life's dazzling options in a time of unparal-
leled prosperity. As presidential candidates Al Gore and
George W. Bush debated how to spend the projected $5
trillion government surplus, Brooks took on the micro-
crisis: How would baby boomers handle the psychic strain
of making money at fulfilling jobs?

"This is the age of discretionary income," Brooks declared, noting that liberal arts majors were "at top income
brackets" and journalists made "six-figure salaries." The
WASP aristocracy that had long ruled the U.S. had been
replaced with a meritocracy based on hard work and cre-

ative prowess. Anyone could join—provided he or she had the right education.

Therein lay the hidden anxiety. According to Brooks, baby boomers had surmounted class and ethnic barriers through the accumulation of credentials. A degree from Harvard now carried more prestige—and provided more opportunity—than the bloodlines that had propelled the Protestant elite.

But the appeal of a college degree was also its fatal flaw: anyone could get it. The formula could only work once, as the same educational system that created new elites now threatened the prospects of their heirs.

"Members of the educated class can never be secure about their children's future," Brooks wrote. "Compared to past elites, little is guaranteed."

He claimed the burden of maintaining success fell on the children themselves, who would have to "work through school" just like their parents.

As it turned out, there was another way.

In the fourteen years since *Bobos* was published, elites have done much to guarantee their children's security. Namely, they have raised the price of the credentials needed to participate in the new meritocracy by such dramatic measures that it locks out a large part of the population while sending nearly everyone else into debt.

Since 2000, the average cost of tuition and fees has more than doubled, while student loan debt has grown at double-digit rates and well-paying jobs have all but vanished. Since 2001, employment in low-wage occupations has increased by 8.7 percent while employment in middle-wage occupations has decreased by 7.3 percent. The most popular industries pay poorly: according to the April 2014 jobs report, four of the top six industries that saw job creation were in the lowest-paying fields. Meanwhile, in prestigious professions, entry-level jobs have been replaced with full-time, unpaid internships.

Today's youth are the best-educated generation in U.S. history. But opportunities are reserved only for those who can buy them. Young U.S. citizens have inherited an entrenched meritocracy that combines the baby boomers' emphasis on education with the class rigidity of the WASP aristocracy it allegedly undermined.

Purchasing Credentials

College does not guarantee a job. It is debatable whether college—in a time of defunded and eliminated programs, rampant grade inflation, and limited student-professor interaction—offers much of an education, at least one for which it is worth taking on significant debt. So why go?

People go to college because not going to college carries a penalty. College is a purchased loyalty oath to an imagined employer. College shows you are serious enough about your life to risk ruining it early on. College is a promise the economy does not keep—but not going to college promises you will struggle to survive.

In an entrenched meritocracy, those who cannot purchase credentials are not only ineligible for most middle-class jobs but are informed that their plight is the result of poor "choices." This ignores that the "choice" of college usually requires walking the road of financial ruin to get the reward—a reward of employment that, in this economy, is illusory.

Credentialism is economic discrimination disguised as opportunity. Over the past forty years, professions that never required a college degree began demanding it.

"The United States has become the most rigidly credentialized society in the world," write James Engell and Anthony Dangerfield in their 2005 book *Saving Higher Education in the Age of Money*. "A BA is required for jobs that by no stretch of the imagination need two years of full-time training, let alone four."

The promotion of college as a requirement for a middle-class life in an era of shrinking middle-class jobs has resulted in an increase in workers whose jobs do not require the degree—15 percent of taxicab drivers, 18 percent of firefighters. More perniciously, it has resulted in the exclusion of the non-college-educated from professions of public influence. In 1971, 58 percent of journalists had a college degree. Today 92 percent do, and at many publications, a graduate degree in journalism is required—despite the fact that most renowned journalists have never formally studied journalism.

Journalism is one of many fields of public influence—including politics—in which credentials function as de facto permission to speak, rendering those who lack them less likely to be employed and less able to afford to stay in their field. Ability is discounted without credentials, but the ability to purchase credentials rests, more often than not, on family wealth.

A "Less Worse" Future

In media and policy circles, this is not how the story is told. A college degree is portrayed as a promise rather than a threat. "People Who Skip College Are Giving Up $800,000 On Average," proclaimed *Business Insider*, one of a slew of publications that portrayed college as the ticket to a near-million-dollar prize.

The $800,000 figure came from a report by the Federal Reserve Bank of San Francisco showing that the average U.S. college graduate will earn at least $800,000 more than the average high school graduate, and that "college is still worth it." The report relied mainly on twentieth-century data, drawing conclusions from a short-lived period in U.S. history when college was cheaper and wages were higher.

That said, the report is not wrong: a college graduate will earn more than a high school graduate. But the real problem is that today both groups earn less and sacrifice more—in time, money, and personal freedom. College does not offer a better future, but a less worse one. College is not a cure for economic insecurity, but a symptom of the broader plague of credentialism.

In an op-ed for *New York* magazine, Benjamin Wallace-Wells cites the popularity of French economist Thomas Piketty to claim that the questions David Brooks and others raised "about the culture of the meritocracy, about what kinds of people got ahead in American life" were "obsolete." America's new language is economics, he writes—oblivious to the fact that economics is, and always has been, the language of meritocracy.

"The Bobo meritocracy will not easily be toppled, even if some group of people were to rise up and conclude that it should be," Brooks wrote in 2000. He is right that it will not be easy. But the first step to toppling a meritocracy is recognizing that it is not a meritocracy. You do not need a college education to know you have been screwed.

—Originally published May 14, 2014

PART V

Media

⌣

Managed Expectations in the Post-Employment Economy

On March 4, Olga Khazan, the new editor of the Global section of *The Atlantic*, sent an email to Nate Thayer, a veteran journalist covering Asian political affairs. Khazan had seen an article Thayer had written about North Korea and liked it. She wanted to know if he could "repurpose" it for the *Atlantic* website.

"We unfortunately can't pay you for it," she wrote Thayer. "But we do reach 13 million readers a month."

Thayer was appalled. He explained that he was a professional journalist "not in the habit of giving my services for free to for-profit media outlets so they can make money by using my work and efforts by removing my ability to pay my bills and feed my children."

Khazan apologized and explained that *The Atlantic* was out of money. She told him the most they paid for an original story was $100, but they did not have $100 at the moment.

All they could offer Thayer was "exposure" to benefit his "professional goals." Thayer's professional goal was to pay his bills. Outraged, he posted the exchange on his blog. It went viral within hours.

Who Pays?

The news that *The Atlantic*—one of the oldest and most venerated publications in America—paid its writers little or nothing came as a shock to many, but not to journalists struggling to make a living in the post-employment economy. Freelance rates have plunged over the past decade, a decline tracked on the crowdsourced website "Who Pays Writers?" (The answer: hardly anyone.)

Some journalists say this is not a big deal. Unpaid labor should be expected, even treasured. In an article called "People Writing for Free on the Internet Is an Enormous Boon to Society," salaried *Slate* columnist Matthew Yglesias argued that if people demanded money for their labor, the world would be deprived of important works. "This Nine Inch Nails/Carly Rae Jepsen mashup is amazing, for example," he wrote.

Atlantic employees say they feel the freelancers' pain, but there is nothing they can do. Editor James Bennet apologized for offending Thayer and added that "when we publish original, reported work by freelancers, we pay them."

This claim was dismissed by *Atlantic* contributors who were paid nothing for their original, reported contributions.

In a lengthy defense of *The Atlantic*'s publishing practices, technology editor Alexis Madrigal argued that while the game of journalism "sucks," it was too late to change the rules: "You still have limited funds. You still can't pay free-lancers a living wage."

But then where is all the money going? "The *Atlantic* is two things every legacy publishing company would like to be: profitable and more reliant on digital advertising revenues than on print," writes *Forbes* magazine. Two thousand twelve brought *The Atlantic* a record profit, beating out its record profit of 2011, with 59 percent of earnings coming from digital revenues. Not every writer at *The Atlantic* is suffering for their craft. When the magazine recruited staff writer Jeffrey Gold-berg, they sent his daughter ponies and offered him a lavish six-figure salary. Thayer had once been offered $125,000 by the magazine to write six articles.

> The economic crisis is a crisis of managed expectations. Americans are being conditioned to accept their own exploitation as normal.

The problem in journalism is not that people are writing for free. It is that people are writing for free for companies that are making a profit. It is that people are doing the same work and getting paid radically disparate wages. It is that corporations making record earnings will not allocate their budgets to provide menial compensation to the workers who make them a success.

The Post-Employment Economy

The Atlantic is far from the only publication to withhold wages, and journalism isn't the only field to do so. In academia, adjunct professors live in poverty doing the same work as the average professor paid $73,207 per year. In many industries—including policy, entertainment, and business—interns do the same jobs as salaried employees and are paid nothing or next to nothing. "We need to hire a 22-22-22," said one new media manager quoted in *The New York Times*, meaning a 22-year-old willing to work 22-hour days for $22,000 a year.

Shortly before the *Atlantic* story broke, a video depicting income inequality in the United States went viral. Based on data from a 2011 study, the video showed that most Americans seek a more equitable distribution of wealth than what they believe exists—but that the reality of income inequality is far worse than they had imagined. When income was graphed, the middle class was barely distinguishable from the poor. Eighty percent of Americans hold 7 percent of the nation's wealth, while 1 percent of Americans hold 40 percent of the nation's wealth.

The video noted that 92 percent of Americans think this is wrong. So why does it continue? The answer lies in a combination of fear and myth-making that has characterized public perception of the economy since the 2008 collapse. Americans are taught to believe the economy is in a permanent crisis—a position seemingly validated by their own experience.

But has the permanent crisis become a self-fulfilling

prophecy? Economic analyst Eric Garland notes that since 2008, executive compensation has steadily risen, but the myth of hard times is peddled to both frighten and lure a permanent supply of unpaid, precarious labor.

"You're only 28. Or 33," he writes, mocking the corporate pitch. "You have a long career ahead of you. *You can get paid later!* After all, we don't have budget for interns this year. We used that money to increase executive pay at a rate five times greater than the cost of living. Because the economy is terrible right now! And we're at all-time record highs of corporate cash reserves and profits. But it's terrible!"

The economic crisis is a crisis of managed expectations. Americans are being conditioned to accept their own exploitation as normal. Ridden with debt from the minute they graduate college, they compete for the privilege of working without pay. They no longer earn money—they earn the prospect of making money. They are paid in "connections" and "exposure." But they should insist on more.

I understand why they do not. When the *Atlantic* story broke, many journalists were tempted to write about their own mistreatment. Some did, but others held back. They did not want to seem angry or ungrateful. They did not want to risk losing what little they had. They were told to pay their dues, and now they are paying for it with their dignity.

In the post-employment economy, is self-respect something we can afford? Or is it another devalued commodity we are expected to give away?

—Originally published March 12, 2013

Who Is a "Journalist"? People Who Can Afford to Be

On September 12, a U.S. Senate panel approved legislation designed to protect journalists from having to reveal their confidential sources. In order to do this, the panel had to define "journalist." According to the proposed law, a journalist is "an employee, independent contractor or agent of an entity that disseminates news or information . . . [who has been] employed for one year within the last 20 years or three months within the last five years."

The definition was met with approval by some and dismay by others. Politico, a website that tracks the minutiae of the D.C. elite, praised it as "a step forward for independent and non-traditional media organizations." The Electronic Frontier Foundation, an organization that seeks to protect free speech online, decried it as offering insufficient protection for independent bloggers, reiterating its earlier argument that "Congress should link shield law protections to the practice of journalism as opposed to the profession."

The Senate debate over who is a "journalist" arose in the aftermath of WikiLeaks, whose activity has been defined as both journalism and espionage. Expanding the definition of a journalist means expanding the legal protection journalists receive.

"I can't support it if everyone who has a blog has a special privilege . . . or if Edward Snowden were to sit down and write this stuff, he would have a privilege. I'm not going to go there," said Senator Dianne Feinstein, in a statement political commentator Matt Drudge denounced as "fascist."

The debate over who is a journalist is a debate over journalistic privilege. But in a prestige economy, the privilege to protect the confidentiality of sources is not the only privilege at play.

Journalism is increasingly a profession only the wealthy can enter. To narrow the definition of "journalist" to those affiliated with established news organizations denies legal protection not only to organizations like WikiLeaks, but also to the writers and bloggers who cannot afford the exorbitant credentials and unpaid internships that provide entry into the trade.

"The journalists who can tell my story—the story of urban or inner-city America—have taken a job in marketing while disseminating their opinions on blogs," writes freelance journalist David Dennis. Since the recession began in 2008, racial diversity in the media has declined while gender imbalance has remained high. The bloggers to whom

Dennis refers would have no legal protection under the Senate's definition.

Whom would the Senate's definition protect? Journalists employed at established publications, who are mainly white men from privileged backgrounds—a category of people who may have little interest in critiquing the establishment that benefits them. The Senate's definition of "journalist" protects the people who need it least.

The Price of Journalism Today

What does it take to succeed in journalism today? For Canadian writer Alexandra Kimball, it was a surprise inheritance. Only after a financial windfall was her freelance career possible.

"To be a writer in this market requires not only money, but a concept of 'work' that is most easily gained from privilege," she writes. "It requires a sense of entitlement . . . and requires you to think of working for free—at an internship, say, or on one of those gratis assignments that seem to be everywhere now—as an opportunity rather than an insult or a scam."

As digital media gave more writers a voice, qualifications for journalism jobs became more stringent and dependent on wealth. This is true worldwide. In 2009, the average cost of journalism school, often a prerequisite for hire in the U.S., was $31,000. Some universities charge over $50,000; along with living expenses the total bill can be above $80,000 (median U.S. household income is $52,000). A British government report showed that in the U.K., journalism is the third most exclusive profession to enter, with the greatest decline in social mobility among its practitioners.

The predominance of privilege has led to a deterioration of journalistic standards. "The people who have time to fool around for no money are the people who already have lots of it," writes journalist James Bloodworth. "And if they are the journalists of the future our media will probably resemble the establishment talking to itself, and if that's the case we will all be worse off, not only us hacks."

Entry-level jobs in journalism have been replaced with full-time internships dependent on other internships. Today people work for the possibility of working, waiting to be considered good enough to be hired by the employers under whom they already labor.

Over the past decade, most internships in journalism have been unpaid. Even *The Nation*, a magazine known for its exemplary coverage of labor exploitation, paid its interns less than minimum wage until the interns protested. They will now make minimum wage—a salary that, in New York City, still locks out the majority of applicants. Only the rich can afford to write about the poor.

Protests against unpaid internships—and unpaid writing, a practice common in publications like *The Atlantic* and the Huffington Post—are on the rise. But the bulk of journalists remain vulnerable. Many lack consistent employment along with health care or a living wage. Now, under the Senate's definition, they may lack legal rights as well.

In an economy this unstable, there is no such thing as a

fixed professional identity. The ability to protect the confidentiality of one's sources should not depend on one.

Unequal Pay

The plight of journalists is emblematic of broader trends in the prestige economy. In multiple professions, workers are performing nearly identical tasks for radically different salaries.

In academia, the tenured professor and the adjunct may teach the same courses and publish in the same journals, but only the latter earns poverty wages. In policy, unpaid interns often write and research the papers for which their well-compensated superiors get credit. And in journalism, freelancers often receive nothing while their staff equivalents earn lavish salaries.

Title may determine whether a journalist will get to maintain the right to confidentiality. But title is an arbitrary measure. It does not show professionalism so much as prestige, ethics so much as affluence and luck.

In an economy in which full-time work has been replaced by part-time labor, it is very easy to lose one's professional affiliation, and the benefits—both material and reputational—it provides. Many do not define themselves as one thing but move in and out of different professions, struggling to find what work they can.

Kelly J. Baker, a well-published PhD working, like most scholars, as an adjunct professor, was told at a conference that she was "not a real academic" because she lacked a tenure-track job. "What the hell was I supposed to say to students now?" she recalls thinking. "Please ignore me as I contemplate my lack of reality? Don't listen to me because I don't matter?"

The Senate's definition of "journalist" applies that same standard to unaffiliated writers and reporters: Do not listen to them, because they do not matter. Do not protect them, because what they offer is not worth protecting—although it may be worth prosecuting.

Credibility is not something that can be bought, but credentials are. Using affiliation as a criterion to define "journalist" means only the privileged get journalistic privilege. The Senate's target may be WikiLeaks, but their proposed ruling gives a de facto demotion to writers locked out for economic reasons.

Journalists of prior generations worked their way up. Today, journalists are expected to start with an elite status and accept wages that have dwindled to nothing.

The result is that journalism is a profession which most Americans cannot afford to formally enter. The Senate should not be able to determine who is a journalist, when the people whom they represent cannot afford to determine that themselves.

—Originally published September 17, 2013

Blame It on the Internet

n June 2013, Prime Minister Recep Tayyip Erdogan announced that Turkey was under threat.

"There is a problem called Twitter right now and you can find every kind of lie there," he told reporters following days of mass protest in Istanbul. "The thing that is called social media is the biggest trouble for society right now."

Days later, twenty-five Twitter users were arrested on charges of inciting demonstrations and spreading propaganda. Officials claimed they used Twitter to organize protests.

"If that's a crime, then we all did it," said Ali Engin, an opposition representative.

Social media was not Erdogan's biggest problem. His biggest problem was that citizens whose lives and nation were harmed by his rule were fighting back, and they had found an effective medium through which to organize and express their protest. Twitter was the problem because its users had identified Erdogan as the problem.

Erdogan is far from the only leader to use "social media" as a stand-in for the people who use it. Repressive regimes ascribe inherent characteristics to the Internet as if it were a contact disease. In Azerbaijan, Facebook gives you "mental problems." In Saudi Arabia, Twitter costs you a spot in the afterlife. In some countries, official denouncement of social media is followed by the arrest of those who use it to criticize officials.

When the powerful condemn the medium of a marginalized messenger, it is the messenger they are truly after. Most recognize that in authoritarian regimes, the demonization of social media is a transparent play for power. Few who see themselves as advocates for justice support the condemnation of those who use it to fight for their rights.

That is why it is startling to see social media portrayed in nearly identical rhetoric by those who claim to support social justice.

"Twitter is a poisonous well of bad faith and viciousness," tweeted *Nation* columnist Katha Pollitt after engaging in Twitter debate with feminists who disagreed with her views. Pollitt's comments were followed up by a *Nation* cover story called "Feminism's Toxic Twitter Wars," which described Twitter as a site of "Maoist hazing" and "perpetual psychodrama."

The article was written by Michelle Goldberg, a journalist, who in December wrote a spirited defense of Justine Sacco, the white PR executive who tweeted a racist joke mocking black Africans dying of AIDS. The antagonists of Goldberg's "Toxic Twitter" were female activists of color, although particular wrath was reserved for Mikki Kendall, a prominent black intellectual best known for starting the hashtag #solidarityisforwhitewomen to highlight the lack of support for women of color in the mainstream feminist community. The hashtag was partly inspired by white feminist defense of Hugo Schwyzer, a writer who had attacked women of color online and confessed to numerous acts of harassment, describing himself as "a breathtakingly cocky fraud" and a "piss-poor feminist."

Nothing about Schwyzer was in Goldberg's article. Instead, Goldberg frequently alluded to Kendall's bad reputation.

"Many consider her a bully, though few want to say so out loud," she wrote in the pages of a magazine to which over 100,000 people subscribe. No "fear" stopped Goldberg from calling Kendall a "bully" in one of the most prominent publications of the American left. But despite the lengthy profile, she could not name a single case of Kendall bullying anyone.

Target the Medium, Slander the Messenger

It is a tactic reminiscent of dictators facing a challenge to power: target the medium, slander the messenger, ignore the message.

What is Kendall's message?

"Feminism as a global movement meant to unite all

women has global responsibilities, and—as illustrated by hundreds of tweets—has failed at one of the most basic: It has not been welcoming to all women, or even their communities," she wrote in *The Guardian* last August.

Since then, she and other female intellectuals of color have used Twitter hashtags to draw attention to social issues like poverty, racism, stereotypes, media bias, and the sexual exploitation of black girls. They were wildly successful, reaching millions of users who appreciated the opportunity to have their struggles acknowledged and their voices amplified.

> *"The thing that is called social media is the biggest trouble for society right now."*

As in any discussion of a contentious issue—online or offline—the conversations from hashtag activism are heated. In the view of Goldberg and others, this renders some women "afraid to speak."

"So glad [Goldberg] wrote about online feminist toxicity in *The Nation*. So many of us are scared to talk about it," tweeted feminist writer Jill Filipovic, who, like Goldberg and others cited in the piece, has a mainstream media platform where she can talk about it regularly.

As I have written, the mainstream media are no different than social media in their callousness and cruelty, and in many ways they are worse because of their perceived legitimacy. In the last few months, mainstream authors have bullied a cancer patient, inspired a transgender woman to commit suicide, and argued that violence against black men is justified. The prestige of old media gives bigoted ranting respectability, recusing the author from consequence.

Social media is viewed by gatekeepers as simultaneously worthless and a serious threat. Balancing these opposing views requires a hypocrisy that can be facilitated only by the assurance of power.

Gatekeepers to mainstream feminist venues, like Jezebel founder Anna Holmes, proclaim that tweeting is not really activism. In contrast, the women behind hashtag activism argue that Twitter is one of the few outlets they have in a world that denies them opportunities to be heard.

"Twitter hashtags happen because the chances of getting real contact and effective representation from our 'leaders' is nonexistent," notes writer and activist Sydette Harry, who tweets as "Blackamazon." Her statement mirrors those of activists around the world who use Twitter to oppose repressive governments.

Twitter activism among black Americans causes discomfort because it highlights the structural nature of racist oppression in the U.S. as well as the complicity of those who uphold and benefit from it. When U.S. journalists cover Twitter activism in other countries, they portray it as empowering. When marginalized people of color—people whose own history of oppression in the U.S. is systematically played down—share their plight online, it is recast as aggression, exaggeration and lies. This, too, mirrors the rhetoric used by dictators around the world.

Rhetoric is not the same as action. But it is the disparate nature of repressive foreign dictatorships and the comparatively open media environment of the U.S. that make the similarity in rhetoric so striking.

Does Twitter Activism Matter?

What does it mean for Twitter activism to "matter"? Four years ago, I wrote about Kyrgyzstan's use of social media during its 2010 uprising, which was dismissed by foreign commentators as unworthy of note. But it was not social media they were dismissing. Kyrgyzstanis used social media to reach other Kyrgyzstanis, but this focus on their own community made them, to outside commentators, impenetrable and irrelevant. The dismissal of Central Asian social media was in fact a dismissal of Central Asians. Western reception—and approval—was viewed as more important than the relevance of the medium for the community in question.

"There isn't a neat separation between the online world and a separate place called the 'real world,'" write activists Mariame Kaba and Andrea Smith in a thoughtful rejoinder to the *Nation* piece. "In the 21st century, these places are one in the same. As such the concept of 'Twitter feminism' strikes us as dismissive and probably a misnomer."

"Twitter activism" is dismissed because the people who engage in it are dismissed—both online and on the ground in Western countries where few minorities hold positions of power. Media is one form of power, and hashtag feminism is an attempt to challenge the narratives that bolster discriminatory practices.

Hashtag feminism makes visible what was never truly invisible, but what people refuse to see. The simultaneous sharing of personal stories is a revelatory process and a bulwark against gaslighting. Our pain matters, the storytellers say, to those who deny their pain ever existed.

In her history *The Warmth of Other Suns,* Pulitzer Prize–winning author Isabel Wilkerson describes the migration of African Americans fleeing the Jim Crow South. She notes that their migration resembled the pattern of those fleeing famine, war, and genocide, despite the fact that African Americans were moving within their own country. This is not a distant history. The protagonists of Wilkerson's book lived in our lifetime, and the legacy of racial violence, segregation, and exclusion they experienced continues into the present.

It is difficult to confront a complex history. It is painful to acknowledge systematic injustice. It is uncomfortable to hear firsthand accounts that contradict the dominant narrative, or that undermine what many would like to believe.

But it is easy to blame the Internet.

—Originally published February 4, 2014

When the Mainstream Media Are
the Lunatic Fringe

On January 8, 2014, Emma Keller, a journalist for *The Guardian*, wrote a column about a woman named Lisa Bonchek Adams. Adams has stage IV breast cancer, and Keller was annoyed.

"As her condition declined, her tweets amped up both in frequency and intensity," complained Keller. "I couldn't stop reading—I even set up a dedicated @adamslisa column in Tweetdeck—but I felt embarrassed at my voyeurism. Should there be boundaries in this kind of experience? Is there such a thing as TMI?"

Keller's column inspired outrage among the thousands of people following Adams's Twitter account, many of them cancer patients who find solace in Adams's words. *Guardian* readers questioned the cruelty of believing the worst thing about pain was that it is too consistently expressed. Why had Keller not simply stopped reading the Twitter account, instead of belittling an ailing stranger? Why would *The Guardian* sanction a column attacking a cancer-stricken mother of three?

But the attack on Adams had only begun.

On January 12, Bill Keller, husband of Emma Keller and the former executive editor of *The New York Times*, wrote his own column chastising Adams for not dying more quietly. He accused her of "raising false hopes" for other cancer patients, and compared her active online presence unfavorably to his "father-in-law's calm death."

Writing about cancer is not new. Under Bill Keller's tenure, numerous *Times* contributors penned articles about their own struggles. But these were different than Adams's Twitter account: they were sanctioned by Keller for print consumption. In Keller's world, mere mortals should not deign to tweet about their mere mortality.

When Keller was pressed by the *Times*' public editor to explain himself, he did not apologize for hurting Adams or for using column space to defend his wife's ill-begotten ideas. He blamed his critics for using Twitter, "a medium [that] encourages reflexes rather than reflection."

Keller's aversion to social media is common among media's old guard, who believe it has eroded standards of ethics and behavior. Outlets like *The Atlantic* regularly run pieces such as "Is Google making us stupid?" or "Is Facebook making us lonely?" (According to researchers, it is not.)

"The medium is the message," Marshall McLuhan famously said. In the digital age, condemning the medium is often shorthand for condemning not only the message but the messenger—and her right to speak. Twitter, which is extremely popular among young African Americans, functions as a public gathering space for marginalized groups to rally under common causes—one of which is countering cruel and inaccurate portrayals of them found in mainstream media.

Old Viciousness, New Visibility

The condemnation of digital media has two sides. There is a legitimate claim that digital media has given old viciousness new visibility, as demonstrated in Amanda Hess's piece on the attacks women receive for writing online. (Hess's piece neglected to include women of color, who arguably experience more vicious harassment than anyone.) Certain facets of social media—speed, anonymity, the ability to "dox"—have changed the nature of harassment, making it easier to accomplish and less likely to be redressed.

But are the mainstream media any different in their biases and cruelty? They do not appear to be. Mainstream media cruelty is actually more dangerous, for it incorporates language that, were it blogged by an unknown, would likely be written off as the irrelevant ramblings of a sociopath.

Instead, the prestige of old media gives bigoted ranting respectability. Even in the digital age, old media define and shape the culture, repositioning the lunatic fringe as the voice of reason.

Shortly after the Kellers' debacle—which resulted in the removal of Emma's piece—a journalist nonchalantly announced that he had prompted the subject of his story to commit suicide. In "Grantland," a blog associated with ESPN, Caleb Hannan profiled a mysterious inventor known as Dr. V. During the course of Hannan's interviews with Dr. V, he learned that she was transgender. Hannan threatened to out her against her will. A few days later, Dr. V committed suicide.

"Writing a eulogy for a person who, by all accounts, despised you is an odd experience," wrote Hannan, in a typically heartless and cavalier passage. Much as cancer patients condemned the Kellers, so did transgender activists condemn Hannan, for an act of cruelty made more incomprehensible by the fact that Hannan's piece was actually published. A woman died for a story, and that, for "Grantland," was okay. A woman suffering from cancer was attacked for suffering the wrong way, and that, for *The New York Times*, was okay.

> In the American media, white people debate whether race matters, rich people debate whether poverty matters, and men debate whether gender matters. People for whom these problems must matter are locked out of the discussion.

It is not surprising that people lack empathy. What is surprising is that unbridled antipathy toward innocent people continues to be sanctioned in an era when fatuous arguments—and terrible ethics—are called out en masse. For critics of mainstream media cruelty, social media is a means to prevent lunacy from being accepted as logic. To the mainstream, it is mere "snark."

Mainstream media cruelty targets those who lack power. Their crime is daring to exist. Along with cancer patients and transgender individuals, racial minorities are a frequent focus.

Over the past year, *Washington Post* columnist Richard Cohen has argued that interracial marriage triggers the "gag reflex" of "conventional Americans" and that young black men like Trayvon Martin deserve to be viewed as suspicious (and by association, shot). This is not an unusual position—one can find similar views on white supremacist websites. But when a mainstream newspaper promotes an extreme viewpoint as normal, it helps make it normal. It sets parameters—"Are interracial relationships repulsive?"—that most Americans would never countenance, and forces us to take them seriously.

This tactic is not limited to newspapers or websites. We find it in book publishing as well. Next month, professors Amy Chua and Jed Rubenfeld are set to release *The Triple Package: How Three Unlikely Traits Explain the Rise and Fall of Cultural Groups in America,* which ranks groups by cultural superiority.

Unsurprisingly, Chua and her husband fall into the most exalted categories: Chinese and Jews. The book is peddled as "scientific," but its hierarchy of peoples is racist propaganda with a careful omission of the word "race." Anthropology's theory of culture, which sought to debunk ethnic stereotypes, is now used by people like Chua to uphold them.

The most interesting thing about Chua's book is that someone agreed to publish it. This is also the most interesting thing about Cohen, Hannan, the Kellers, or the innumerable mainstream media publishers who trade on biases most find repugnant. Some have attributed this to a search for clicks and traffic—"hate-reading" as profitable pastime. But there is a broader question here: that of legitimacy.

Disproportionate Influence

Sociologist Zeynep Tufekci has called the Internet "a public sphere erected on private property." All voices can speak, but only few are heard. Amplification is tied to prestige, meaning that where you publish—and what privileges you already have—gives your words disproportionate influence.

The terms of public debate are rarely set by the public. "Inequality" has risen to the fore in pundit discourse, but mostly in terms of whether it deserves to be debated at all, as recent columns by the *Washington Post*'s Ezra Klein and *The New York Times*' David Brooks demonstrate. For a public well aware of income inequality—since they have to live with its consequences every day—such debates reflect an inequality of their own: a paucity of understanding among our most prominent voices.

In the American media, white people debate whether race matters, rich people debate whether poverty matters, and men debate whether gender matters. People for whom these problems must matter—for they structure the limitations of their lives—are locked out of the discussion.

In January 2014, Suey Park, an Asian-American activist,

was asked by the Huffington Post to help curate an "Asian Voices" section that would bring prominence to underrepresented Asian Americans. She was thrilled—until she was informed her contributors would not be paid a dime. Disgusted, Park rejected their offer and took to Twitter with the hashtag #ExploitedVoices.

The hashtag was meant to highlight how minorities are priced out of journalism, but it aptly captures the ethos of our times. In the mainstream media, exploited voices are meant to be seen—and criticized, and chastised, and caricatured for clicks and cash. But rarely are they heard.

—Originally published January 22, 2014

PART VI

Beyond Flyover Country

U.S. Foreign Policy's Gender Gap

The dearth of women in U.S. foreign policy is a subject of continual interest, mostly because it never changes. According to a 2011 survey by policy analyst Micah Zenko, women make up less than 30 percent of senior positions in the government, military, academy, and think tanks.

As of 2008, 77 percent of international relations faculty and 74 percent of political scientists were men. In international relations literature, women are systematically cited less than men.

The majority of foreign policy bloggers and the vast majority of op-ed writers—with estimates ranging from 80 to 90 percent—are men. When lists of intellectuals are made, women tend to appear in a second-round, outrage-borne draft. Female intellectuals gain prominence through tales of their exclusion. They are known for being forgotten.

People talk about the glass ceiling, but it is really a glass box. Everyone can see you struggling to move. There is an echo in the glass box as your voice fails to carry. You want to talk about it, but that runs the risk of making all people hear.

Balancing Career with Motherhood

Before the summer of 2012, Anne-Marie Slaughter was best known as an international relations theorist and advisor to Secretary of State Hillary Clinton. She is now best known for detailing the difficulty of balancing her career with motherhood in her *Atlantic* cover story "Why Women Still Can't Have It All."

The essay describes Slaughter's decision to resign her State Department post for her teaching position at Princeton, which allowed her more time with her children, and argues that the inability of women to rise to power has less to do with a lack of ambition than a lack of structural support. It is the most-shared article in *The Atlantic*'s history.

Obviously the success of the article does not diminish Slaughter's achievements in international relations. But younger women in the field could likely not publish such a personal piece and remain respected. The most radical thing about Slaughter's article is that she wrote it at all.

Slaughter, the all-star, took one for the team (although who the team is, given Slaughter's elite circles, remains up for debate). This was possible because her accomplishments already trumped her gender in terms of her public reputation, if not in her private life. She was seen as a person, so she could afford to be seen as a woman.

Slaughter's article resonated with many younger women trying to succeed in competitive fields. But her own field, international relations, remains one of the most lopsided, gender-wise. Year after year, the imbalance is decried.

What accounts for women's exclusion? There are two problems.

The first is perception, which translates into respect. The second is money, which translates into opportunity. The first problem is a gender problem (and a race problem). But the second problem is shared by everyone—or almost everyone. It is the "almost" that is itself the problem.

A Self-Selecting Community

The foreign policy community is suffering from what national security fellow Faris Alikhan calls "credential creep." Credential creep, he writes, is the stockpiling of prestigious degrees and experiences to differentiate oneself from the increasingly esteemed competition. But these accolades come at a price too high for the average person to pay.

An MA in foreign policy can run a person tens of thousands of dollars into debt, and the expectation that one's initial labor—whether in internships, fellowships, or writing contributions—will go unpaid limits participation in the field. Cities of power like D.C. have become unaffordable for most people. As a result, Alikhan argues, the U.S.

foreign policy community is looking a lot like the Song dynasty.

"The next generation of foreign policy leaders is socialized in a hyper-competitive bubble, while voices from lower-income and minority groups are seldom heard since they can't afford to compete," he writes. "In essence, those who aspire to affect one of the most important aspects of our nation—our relationship to the rest of the world—are part of a self-selecting community of those whose families are wealthy enough for them to develop credentials and connections."

Money, not gender, is the biggest barrier to a career in international relations, or any prestige industry. It eliminates the bulk of the talent pool from the start. Building a career in policy often means not only living on little income, but paying your way around the world.

Nowadays, candidates for internships at *The Economist* must be able to fly to London merely to interview. Interning at the United Nations means relocating temporarily, unpaid, to expensive cities. Foreign policy was always an elite profession, but the cost of entry has skyrocketed.

There are ways around this. Writing, for example, is an inexpensive way to get out your ideas and build a reputation. But here a woman runs into a second problem: perception.

List of Indignities

Every woman working in an intellectual field has her list of indignities. Mine include being called a "mom blogger" by *USA Today*, despite having never written about my children; having questions about my research directed to the male scholars sitting next to me at conferences; and the constant assumption that I study "women from Central Asia." (I reply that I study people from Central Asia, and then awkwardly explain that women fall into this category.)

Hiding behind a computer screen seems an effective way to dodge gender bias. Sometimes the reader bypasses your byline and accidentally respects you, culminating in an email of praise.

But other times you find what political scientist Charli Carpenter described, in the midst of a blogging controversy, as a "power dynamic to engage in actual, deliberate, blatant, sexist, sexualized, public disparagement of me and other female scholars and public intellectuals over the years as a way of dismissing our ideas when we dare to make a mistake or are simply politically unpopular."

On the Internet, everyone knows you are a woman.

The online atmosphere Carpenter depicts has been commented upon by many female writers, but endured quietly by more. To discuss how you are negatively perceived forces people to see you through your detractor's eyes. To discuss sexism is to invite pity, to be reduced, even in support, to something less than what you are. When you work in the realm of ideas and trade in the currency of respect, this is a tough balance to pull off—and it goes hand in hand with the tough balance Slaughter describes of career and family.

Parents of both genders are discriminated against in any field that requires unpaid work, inflexible hours, and frequent travel. But it is a simple truth that mothers bear these burdens more. They pay the highest financial toll, turning down opportunities as the cost of child care soars and salaries stagnate. They also endure a greater stigma for discussing it.

In the glass box, a statement of fact sounds like a complaint. In a tough job market, a complaint can be a career killer. Discussing gender bias can be mistaken as a plea for tokenism. It seems safer to downplay structural problems—and the subjective subtleties of discrimination—for a more uplifting take.

Breaking Down Barriers

What results is an argument that women bring something special to foreign affairs that necessitates their inclusion—not as people, but as women. Arguing that women should be hired because, well, that seems fair, lacks the imperative force needed to undermine gender hierarchies and unjust economic structures. Instead, the grounds for exclusion are marketed as virtue.

Countless think tanks have issued statements, like this from the National Democracy Institute: "Democracy cannot truly deliver for all of its citizens if half of the population remains underrepresented in the political arena."

The notion that representation by women in the political arena will necessarily lead to democracy has been refuted, both on a national level (dictatorial Belarus, Uzbekistan, and Kazakhstan have the highest representation of women in parliament) and on an individual one (think: Thatcher,

Palin). But in the end, it does not matter whether you believe that being female makes you particularly diplomatic, or empathetic, or kind.

It matters whether you believe women are as capable of the job as men, whether you believe capable women deserve the job as much as capable men, and whether you act on this belief or let the ratio rest.

U.S. foreign policy needs workers with a greater diversity of skills, ideas, and experience. This means not only including more women, but working against the economic barriers that deter many talented young people—male and female—from entering the field.

If you need convincing that foreign policy needs new blood, look at the state of the world around you. The strongest argument against the status quo is the status quo itself.

—*Originally published March 20, 2014*

Snowden and the Paranoid State

Paranoids are not paranoid because they're paranoid," Thomas Pynchon wrote in *Gravity's Rainbow*, "but because they keep putting themselves, fucking idiots, deliberately into paranoid situations."

On June 23, 2013, Edward Snowden left China, a repressive state with a vast surveillance system, to fly to Russia, a repressive state with an even vaster surveillance system, in order to escape America, where he had worked for a surveillance system so vast he claims it gave him "the power to change people's fates."

In proclaiming his ability to change the fates of others, Snowden lost control of his own. He was lambasted as the instigator of international conspiracies and praised as the source of their revelation. He was at once a hero and a traitor, a pawn and a king, a courageous whistle-blower with the means to bring down nations and a naive narcissist, little millennial lost.

What are people looking for when they look at Snowden? They are looking for answers about how much states and corporations know about their personal lives, but more than that, they are looking for a sense that answers are possible. They are looking for knowledge untainted by corruption, as Snowden continues his world tour of corrupt regimes. They are looking for state agendas explained by someone without an agenda of his own. They are looking, and they are not finding what they seek.

Snowden's Legacy

Satisfactory explanations require trust in the person explaining. In the long term, Snowden will be seen as a symptom of breakdown in political trust, not a cause. His legacy is paranoia—the paranoia of the individual about the paranoia of the state that spurs the paranoia of the public. This is not to say that paranoia is always unjustified. But it has become a weltanschauung instead of a reaction.

It matters, of course, whether the allegations of mass surveillance and data-collecting made by Snowden and *Guardian* writer Glenn Greenwald are true, but this is not what determines how the allegations are received. Suspicion of surveillance can be as poisonous to a functioning democracy as surveillance itself. Not knowing the extent of surveillance—of whom, by whom, to what end—heightens anxiety over the distance between the powerful and the public, an anxiety that was in place long before Snowden emerged.

Between the state and the citizen, we have the media, whose biases and careerism thicken the fog. With Snowden, every revelation has a refutation, but citizens are left to evaluate the state of their nation based on their trust in the individual reporting it.

Months into the scandal, it has become clear the Snowden beat tends toward the tautological. If a writer believes—or finds it advantageous to proclaim—that NSA employees respect the citizen's right to privacy and the legal codes that protect him or her, then Snowden's claims are unfounded exaggerations. If a writer believes—or finds it advantageous to proclaim—that NSA employees are prone to abuse the system they have created, and that the government will lie to protect its creation, then Snowden's claims are evidence of systemic abuse.

You do not need a database to watch Americans suffer.

"Sometimes paranoia's just having all the facts," wrote William S. Burroughs. And sometimes paranoia is the broken belief that having the facts is possible.

When Anxiety Attacks

American political paranoia has a long history, perhaps most famously summed up in Richard Hofstadter's study of the "paranoid style in American politics," in which he described how a small minority employed theories that were "overheated, oversuspicious, overaggressive, grandiose, and apocalyptic in expression," often gaining power in the process.

Hofstadter's study was published in 1965, thirty years before the popularization of an international communications system that potentially gives every citizen the ability to debunk fatuous claims and distribute reliable evidence. The Internet would seem an antidote to conspiracy theories and state secrecy, but it has only amplified both.

Paranoia is aggression masked as defense. It was paranoia (and hubris, and greed) that caused the run-up to the Iraq War; it is paranoia that leads to thousands of innocent Muslims being profiled in New York; it is paranoia that led to Trayvon Martin being shot to death on the street. In Congress, paranoia is less a style than a sickness, employed less with flourish than with fear. Paranoia is the refusal to recognize others except as filtered through ourselves—and how do Americans see themselves? Afraid, afraid, afraid.

Digital transparency changes politics, but also reinforces what aspects of politics seem resistant to change. When WikiLeaks released its cables two years ago, they did not impart shocking new information so much as confirm people's worst suspicions.

One of the most disconcerting aspects of a massive spy system is how little all that information does to remedy corruption and incompetence. Big Brother is scary not just because he knows so much, but because he is capable of so little.

Snowden came of age in a paranoid era. The Bush administration was marked by twin delusions: hysteria over terrorism, abetted by an insistence on defining reality contrary to evidence, and self-congratulation on triumphs never achieved: Hurricane Katrina relief efforts characterized as a "heck of a job," the war in Iraq characterization as "mission accomplished," and the bubble economy.

Obama ran as an alternative not only to Bush policies, but to the Bush mind-set, offering "hope and change" as antidotes to delusion and intransigence. He inherited the Bush administration's problems at the same time social media networks like Facebook gave powerful people new means of exploring the data of our lives—and of exploring our lives as data.

The fear that the government was inventing justifications to persecute citizens turned into a fear that they were justifying persecution by manipulating data that we did, in fact, produce. We create the trail, but they determine where it originates and leads. This is the anxiety that propels Snowden's revelations.

A Culture of Paranoia

But the deeper fear, the real sadness, is that ordinary people are insignificant to the government, and that those in power are indifferent to our fate. You do not need a database to watch Americans suffer.

The Obama administration espouses moving rhetoric about some of our biggest problems—unemployment, violence, and inequality—but has had little success in solving them. Its frenetic pursuit of Snowden is remote from ordinary life. Citizens only feel the repercussions in paranoia, a grasp at self-importance despite all evidence to the contrary.

On July 31, journalist Michele Catalano became convinced that a Google search for "pressure cooker" and "backpacks" had caused a "joint terrorism task force" to pay a visit to her home. In reality, it was not a terrorism task force but the local Long Island police. They did not come because a cadre of distant observers had access to her Internet search history but because her husband's former employer had asked them to investigate activity her husband had conducted on his work computer. As Gawker's Adrien Chen writes, "The actually scary part of Catalano's story—the creepy correlation of Google history in some distant control room—started, and ended, in her imagination."

Fixing the NSA scandal will involve far more than reforming the NSA. It means changing America's paranoid political culture, which means reviving trust in our leaders, which means finding leaders deserving of trust. It means that people in positions of power—in government and in corporations like Facebook and Google—need to come clean with what they know and why they want to know it. Our privacy settings, literally and figuratively, need to stop shifting. Our privacy expectations need to stop being dictated by those who read our mail.

Until then, paranoia will rule. "Power is impenetrable," wrote Elias Canetti, in his 1960 study of paranoia in politics.

"The man who has it sees through other men, but does not allow them to see through him."

Edward Snowden proclaimed he could see through everybody. And then he said he was on our side. That is the novelty of this whole affair. He saw through us and we watched him run.

—Originally published August 5, 2013

Iraq and the Reinvention
of Reality

The worst thing about the Iraq war was not that people got away with lying. It was that they did not—and it did not matter.

The tenth anniversary of the American invasion of Iraq was a week of media culpa. Every day a new journalist or pundit came forward to atone for supporting a war predicated on disinformation. "I was excitable and over-reacted," wrote blogger Andrew Sullivan, explaining why he once argued that no "serious person" could doubt Saddam Hussein's intent to use WMDs with his co-conspirator al-Qaeda. "I owe readers an apology for being wrong on the overriding question of whether the war made sense," wrote journalist David Ignatius, noting that, in retrospect, it did not.

The media's failure to question the fallacies of the Bush administration has long been derided—as *The Nation*'s Greg Mitchell noted, they have been apologizing for years. But while it is right to criticize the media, it is wrong to hold them completely accountable. Plenty of people got Iraq wrong, but plenty of people—experts and ordinary citizens— got it right. The problem was that it made no difference.

"Without evidence, confidence cannot arise," Hans Blix declared to the United Nations in the run-up to the war. He was wrong: confidence, like evidence, could be created. The warnings of Blix, Anthony Zinni, Mohamed ElBaradei, the liberal columnists called out as fifth columnists, and the hundreds of thousands of protesters around the world changed nothing. When revelation hit, it was with a sense of helplessness that defined the decade to come. Confidence, like evidence, could be destroyed.

The Iraq war is notable not only for journalistic weakness, but for journalistic futility: the futility of fact itself. Fact could not match the fabrications of power. Eventually, our reality shifted to become what they conceived. "I could have set myself on fire in protest on the White House lawn and the war would have proceeded without me," wrote Bush speechwriter David Frum.

That was the message of the Iraq war: there is no point in speaking truth to power when power is the only truth.

The Flavor of Our Time

In 2002, Ron Suskind, a reporter for *The New York Times*, met with an unnamed aide to George W. Bush who accused Suskind of being part of the "reality-based community." The aide meant it as an insult: this was not the way the world worked anymore.

"We're an empire now, and when we act, we create our own reality," said the aide, later alleged to be Bush adviser Karl Rove. "And while you're studying that reality— judiciously, as you will—we'll act again, creating other new realities, which you can study too, and that's how things will sort out. We're history's actors . . . and you, all of you, will be left to just study what we do."

> *Fact could not match the fabrications of power. Eventually, our reality shifted to become what they conceived.*

In one sense, this quote seems of a piece with its era— with the entry of "truthiness" into the dictionary; with the rise of entire industries, like reality TV, built on choreographed sincerity. But while we may associate the "creation of reality" with a wildly hubristic administration, it remains the flavor of our time, a manipulation that moves from crisis to crisis.

Ten years after the Iraq war, we continue to live in an era of hysterical panic about invented catastrophes and false reassurances about real catastrophes. We laugh bitterly at the "Mission Accomplished" sign raised nearly a decade before the war ended, but the Bush administration did accomplish something. They accomplished the mission of persuading everyday Americans that the unthinkable is normal.

We see remnants of this created reality in the financial

crisis—the ongoing "great recession" that, like preemptive war, has transformed what Americans will accept. It is normal for criminal financiers to receive record bonuses in an age marked by austerity, it is normal for professionals to work years unpaid in the hope of someday landing a job, it is normal for one year of college to cost more than the average median income. This is normal, they say—but if Iraq should have taught us anything, it is how easily and brazenly "normal" can be redefined.

Iraq showed us that the consequences for gross negligence were less than anyone had imagined. This gaping disconnect between people and power, and the public's resignation to adjusting to injustices rather than challenging them, has shaped the postwar era. If Iraq was launched on the illusion of invincibility, the financial crisis is abetted by the acceptance of powerlessness.

We Lost Accountability

On March 18, 2013, Tomas Young, a soldier who was paralyzed fighting in the Iraq war, published a letter from his deathbed:

"I write this letter, my last letter, to you, Mr. Bush and Mr. Cheney. I write not because I think you grasp the terrible human and moral consequences of your lies, manipulation and thirst for wealth and power. I write this letter because, before my own death, I want to make it clear that I, and hundreds of thousands of my fellow veterans, along with millions of my fellow citizens, along with hundreds of millions more in Iraq and the Middle East, know fully who you are and what you have done.

You may evade justice but in our eyes you are each guilty of egregious war crimes, of plunder and, finally, of murder, including the murder of thousands of young Americans—my fellow veterans—whose future you stole."

Tomas Young is thirty-three. (Editor's note: Young died on November 10, 2014.) When he was twenty-one, he decided to protect the country he loved by enlisting in the armed forces. Like his fellow soldiers, he came of age in an era marked by a socioeconomic gulf between the people who agitate for wars and the people who fight them. Like his fellow soldiers, he returned home to a country that denies veterans adequate health services or financial support. Because it is a recession, because times are tough. Because this is normal.

After September 11, 2001, President Bush drew criticism for calling on Americans to go shopping rather than relinquish comforts in a time of war. Young's generation was not told to sacrifice—instead, they were the sacrifice. They paid the price with their lost opportunities, with their lost voice, with their defaulted investment in their nation.

We lost more in Iraq than a war. We lost accountability and faith in our institutions, and most of all, we lost the outrage that accompanies that loss, because we came to expect it and accept it as normal. This quiet acquiescence is, in the end, as damaging as any lie we were told.

—*Originally published March 24, 2013*

Where Following the
Law Is Radical

I n May 2005, the government of Uzbekistan fired on a massive protest in the city of Andijon, killing over seven hundred of its own citizens. Within weeks, a joke began to circulate on Uzbek Internet forums. It went something like this:

Q: Can an Uzbek participate in a demonstration
in Uzbekistan?
A: Yes, but only once.

While meant to mock the brutality of the government of Islam Karimov, who has ruled Uzbekistan since its Soviet days, the joke is also a pointed jab at Uzbekistan's legal system. In Uzbekistan, citizens are arrested, tortured, and even killed for carrying out acts permitted by law. Uzbekistan advertises itself as a democracy, and has a constitution guaranteeing freedom of expression and the protection of human rights. When citizens act on their constitutional rights by criticizing officials or organizing nonviolent protests, the government is quick to arrest them.

Uzbekistan is one of many states in Central Asia where the rule of law has eroded. This is not to say that these states are unstable: the cruel irony of illegality in Central Asia is that it is a stabilizing force. In Uzbekistan corruption at the state level is so pervasive that contesting state crimes is extremely difficult; corruption at the local level is so rampant that it has led to apathy among citizens, who are often unaware of their rights. But the existence of those rights raises an interesting question: What if people retained their faith in law after they lost their faith in government? What if citizens took the law at its word?

In 2010, a group of Uzbek lawyers created a website attempting to do just that. "Adolat" ("justice," in Uzbek) was established with the goal of raising legal literacy among Uzbek citizens and, in doing so, improving the rule of law in Uzbekistan. "Adolat" is not asking that laws be changed, only that they be followed by state officials as well as citizens.

Justice as Radical Subversion?

The founders of "Adolat" are adamant that they are not an opposition group and that they have no interest in upending the existing constitutional system—in fact, they have featured President Karimov's statements on the importance of the law on their website. Despite its apolitical agenda, "Adolat" has been banned. In Uzbekistan, showing people how to follow the law constitutes an act of radical subversion.

It is no mystery why Uzbeks are forbidden to read "Adolat." The website asks Uzbek citizens to buy into a delusion: that they live in a just society where laws are something other than words on a piece of paper. By pretending that laws have meaning, they implore the government to give them meaning—a step which the Karimov regime seems unwilling to take. The legal experts of "Adolat" encourage discussion of civic issues and answer questions submitted by readers. (Sample query: "Where can I complain about abuse by the police?") A lawyer who works for "Adolat" told me that the goal is not to "give fish" but to teach Uzbeks to "fish for themselves." He believes a regular reader of the site should by now be well versed in writing an official complaint.

The Internet is often derided as a medium of inherent inaccuracy, the phrase "But I read it on the Internet!" a punch line. But for "Adolat," the Internet serves as a way to turn Uzbekistan's lip-service law into something sincere—an inversion of Uzbekistan's cynical political culture, which extends to the Uzbek language itself.

Uzbek legal language implies that justice is an arbitrary construct. In layman's terms, a defense attorney is an *oqlovchi*, literally a "whitener," and a prosecutor is a *qoralovchi*, or "darkener." Uzbek lawyers "whiten" or "darken" the *aybdor*—a term which means "defendant" but literally translates as "the guilty one." Justice is reduced to theatrics and spin, fodder for jokes and sarcasm. The grim practices of Uzbekistan's legal system underline this fact. One Uzbek former state official, when I asked him to define "guilt," told me to look up "suspicious"—because "in reality, suspicious is the same as guilty."

A Growing Trend in Central Asia

In contrast, "Adolat" takes care to explicate Uzbekistan's legal code as well as introduce Uzbeks to unfamiliar legal concepts. A recent article was titled "Presumption of innocence [in Uzbek, literally "guiltlessness"]: a history and explanation"—a concept foreign to Uzbekistan in both theory and practice.

"Presumption of innocence" is one of many terms pertaining to law and politics entered into Uzbek language via the Internet. Several years ago, the Birdamlik Movement, an Uzbek opposition group, tried to bring the phrase "nonviolent protest" into Uzbek online discourse. The term was met with confusion not because Uzbek protest is violent, but because it is almost nonexistent. One Uzbek, after reading the definition, asked whether a protest would still be considered nonviolent after the government had killed the protesters.

The efforts of "Adolat" are part of a growing trend in Central Asia of citizens filling in where their states have failed. In Tajikistan, lawyers have created a similar online service for citizens to seek advice on legal affairs. In Kyrgyzstan, Kazakhstan, Tajikistan, and to a lesser extent, Uzbekistan, volunteer organizations have emerged to carry out civic acts the governments fail to accomplish: rebuilding infrastructure, providing child care, and issuing loans. While many of these informal groups have been criticized by state officials, their numbers continue to grow. One analyst credits this trend to "a spirit of civic volunteerism that has existed in Central Asia for centuries."

And that is the tragedy of this situation. A new class of young, enterprising Central Asians has emerged, committed to the rule of law and ready to serve their countrymen—if their governments would only let them.

—Originally published June 14, 2012

Water Is a Human Right, But Who Is Considered a Human Being?

Water is a basic human right.

Few dispute this. From the Talmud to the Bible to the Quran, from the European Federation of Public Service Unions to the United Nations, societies throughout history have recognized water as a public good. To treat water as a commodity instead of a right is an act of violence. In May 2014, UN Secretary General Ban Ki-moon argued that "preventing people's access to safe water is a denial of a fundamental human right." He added: "Deliberate targeting of civilians and depriving them of essential supplies is a clear breach of international humanitarian and human rights law."

Water is a right for all human beings. The question is: Who counts as a human being?

Not the poorest residents of Detroit, a U.S. city which has cut off water to citizens at a rate of three thousand people per week since the spring, totaling about 125,000 people at present. Local activists estimate that up to 300,000 people—nearly all poor and African American—will ultimately lose access to water. The reason for the cut, officials claim, is that residents cannot pay their water bills, which have spiked 120 percent in the last decade.

Detroit is one of the poorest cities in one of the wealthiest countries in the world. Detroit is also surrounded by the largest supply of fresh water in the world. The U.S. does not lack for money, and Detroit does not lack for accessible water. What Detroit lacks are people viewed as worthy of the compassion and resources given to their richer, whiter peers. They lack the rights and respect most U.S. citizens take for granted.

At a rally in June, lifelong Detroiter Renla Session spoke out for her community: "These are my fellow human beings. If they threatened to cut off water to an animal shelter, you would see thousands of people out here. It's senseless . . . They just treat people like their lives mean nothing here in Detroit, and I'm tired of it."

When rights are considered privileges, only the privileged have rights.

"They treat people like animals in Detroit," an autoworker complained in July, but the U.S. treats its poorest citizens worse. When the government shut down in late 2013, the food program for impoverished women and children was suspended—but the animals in the National Zoo stayed fed. More attention was paid to the shutdown of the Panda

Cam, a livestream of a bear cub, than to the suffering of America's poorest citizens.

Water is a human right, but who is a human being? Corporations, the U.S. Supreme Court ruled in June, as the parched citizens of Detroit started filling up at water fountains.

"In its last day in session, the high court not only affirmed corporate personhood but expanded the human rights of corporations, who by some measures enjoy more protections than mortals—or 'natural persons,'" wrote Dana Milbank at the *Washington Post*.

The mortals of Detroit enjoy no such protection. Perhaps that is why the city's corporate venues—like its high-end golf club, hockey arena, football stadium, and over half of the city's commercial and industrial users—still have their water running despite owing over $30 million, while its most impoverished residents have their water, and their rights, taken away.

In Detroit, corporations are people. Their worth is unquestioned because it is measured in dollars. The worth of the residents of Detroit is measured in utility, and so their utilities are denied.

War on Poverty

Human rights may be guaranteed by law, but one's humanity is never a given. The U.S. was built on the labor of slaves considered three-fifths of a person. Today, one's relative humanity—and the rights that accompany it—is shaped by race, class, gender, and geography. Citizens may be subject to the same written laws, but they are not equally subject to the same punishments and practices. Water is a litmus test of how much of a "person" you are considered to be.

For decades, marginalized peoples of the United States have struggled with lack of access to water. Today nearly 40 percent of the 173,000 Navajo, the largest Native American tribe, do not have a tap or a toilet at home. The people of Appalachia, a historically impoverished region of the U.S., were a focal point of the 1960s War on Poverty after their lack of basic public services was publicized.

"This legislation marks the end of an era of partisan cynicism toward human want and misery," President Lyndon Johnson proclaimed in 1965. "Wherever we have our commitments, whether to the old and the strong or to the young and the weak, we shall match our words with deeds."

In January 2014, Freedom Industries, a chemical and mining company, dumped a toxic chemical into the Elk River, poisoning the water for up to 300,000 residents of West Virginia. Hundreds were hospitalized. Locals were shocked, but not surprised, by the horror that ensued. It was West Virginia's fifth major industrial accident in eight years.

"Charleston's nickname is Chemical Valley, and our life expectancy rates reflect this, even in the diaspora," wrote West Virginia writer Cheyenna Layne Weber of the state's capital. "Environmental injustice and trauma become part of your veins and cells, enamel and marrow, and it permeates the economies which underpin our existence. I have tried, but you can't outrun a system."

When the water crisis hit West Virginia, many were horrified, but others mocked the impoverished state—including Detroit journalist Zlati Meyer, unaware her city was next. President Johnson's War on Poverty long ago turned into a war on the poor, and residents of both places have been blamed for their own plight. They elect bad leaders and support corrupt companies, people said of West Virginia. They should have paid their bills, people say of Detroit.

Which leads to the question: So what? Then they should not drink or bathe? They should swallow poison or roam the streets in search of water fountains? Their children, who have no stake in this battle, are supposed to suffer, and their parents are supposed to watch? Is that the lesson we are passing on—that poor children are inherently undeserving of a basic provision in one of the richest countries in the world?

A Third World Problem?

U.S. citizens denied clean water often compare their situation with that of distant, disenfranchised lands.

"It's frightening, because you think this is something that only happens somewhere like Africa," a mother in Detroit told the *LA Times*. "It's like we're living in a Third World country," a West Virginian told *The New Yorker*.

The circumstances differ, but the outcome is the same. Water is a right, and denial of water is a form of social control.

In Ukraine, water and electricity were cut off in certain regions following the Russian incursion. In Syria, multiple political groups manipulated the water supply at different times, leaving roughly one million people without access to clean water or sanitation.

In Gaza, hundreds of thousands of Palestinians lack water, including those living in hospitals and refugee camps. On July 15, citizens of Detroit held a rally in solidarity, holding signs that said, "Water for all, from Detroit to Palestine." A basic resource has become a distant dream, a longing for a transformation of politics aimed at ending suffering instead of extending it.

Water is a legal right ignored in places where law is selectively enforced. To merit the protection of the law one must be acknowledged fully as a human being. What the water crisis shows is who is considered human—and who is considered disposable.

—Originally published July 23, 2014

The Telegenically Dead

n the beginning, they were the "telegenically killed." That is what Charles Krauthammer, in his July 17 *Washington Post* column, "Moral Clarity in Gaza," called the victims of Israeli airstrikes. Children shelled while playing on the beach, a father holding a plastic bag of his two-year-old son's remains: To Krauthammer, Palestinians are not people but production values. War does not destroy families; it "produces dead Palestinians for international television."

Three days later, Prime Minister Benjamin Netanyahu proclaimed the Palestinians "telegenically dead," lifting Krauthammer's language in one example of the U.S. media–Israeli government echo chamber that has been reverberating all summer. "You forfeit your right to be called civilians," a *Wall Street Journal* columnist told Gazans on July 21, stating that children of Hamas supporters are fair game. "There is no such thing as 'innocent civilians,'" proclaimed Giora

Eiland, the former head of Israel's National Security Council, on August 5.

Unthinkable sentiment has become sanctioned, commonplace. You begin to have nostalgia for disappointment, because at least that means you had expectations.

Who are the telegenically dead? The telegenically dead are the dead, plain and simple. That we see them is the novelty, that we grieve them is human, and to be human, today, is a hostile act. To grieve is to acknowledge loss, to acknowledge loss is to affirm life, to affirm life is to contemplate how it was taken.

A child is not a shield or a lawn to be mowed. "Telegenic" means you see a body where you were supposed to see an abstraction.

Inconvenient Death

In 1960, Elie Wiesel published *Night,* a memoir of the Holocaust that portrayed, in intimate and graphic detail, Nazi cruelty and public complicity.

"Was I still alive? Was I awake?" Wiesel wrote, describing Nazis throwing Jewish babies into a bonfire. "I could not believe it. How could it be possible for them to burn people, children, and for the world to keep silent? No, none of this could be true."

In July 2014, Wiesel took out a full-page ad in *The New York Times* to support Israel in what he termed "a battle of civilization versus barbarism." As Palestinians stored corpses of babies killed by Israeli strikes in ice cream freezers, Wiesel proclaimed that "Jews rejected child sacrifice 3,500 years ago. Now it's Hamas' turn." He condemned the "terrorists who have taken away all choice from the Palestinian children of Gaza."

He is right. The Palestinian children of Gaza do not have a choice. But Israel does.

Hamas is a violent organization that commits reprehensible acts. But it was not Hamas who killed Palestinian children playing on the beach. It was not Hamas who killed children sleeping in UN shelters. To argue, as many U.S. and Israeli authors have, that merely being in the proximity of Hamas renders one a legitimate target is terrorist logic— particularly in Gaza, where there is nowhere else to go. In what other "hostage situation" are the hostages targeted— and their deaths justified by stripping away their civilian status, their innocence, their humanity?

A baby killed by soldiers is a baby killed by soldiers. It is not a shield and not a pawn. The death of any child is a tragedy regardless of that child's race, religion, or parentage. That this is debated is its own tragedy.

In 1941, Nazi official Joseph Goebbels complained that Jewish children captivated too much public sympathy: "One suddenly has the impression that the Berlin Jewish population consists only of little babies whose childish helplessness might move us, or else fragile old ladies. The Jews send out the pitiable."

Three years later, the Nazis sent the teenage Wiesel to a concentration camp.

Let me be clear: what is happening in Gaza is in no way

comparable to the Holocaust in scope, scale, organization, or intent. Yet similar rhetoric portraying dead children as complicit or inconvenient emerges—rhetoric not unique to the Middle East, but used all over the world, all throughout history, to mitigate or justify the slaughter of innocents. One would hope that those who so vividly documented the killing of children would protest it being practiced. That hope seems in vain.

"Those who cannot remember the past are condemned to repeat it," George Santayana famously said. Those who can, repeat it, too.

Who Is Human?

Social media has been described as "humanizing" the Palestinian victims. Television may be decried by politicians and pundits, but the Internet is where Gaza's story is told firsthand by its residents, where graphic images of the grieved are shared.

If you are being "humanized," you are already losing. To be "humanized" implies that your humanity is never assumed, but something you have to prove.

"What am I supposed to do/be to be qualified as a human?" Maisam Abumorr, a writer and student in Gaza, asks. "As far as I can tell, I live like normal humans do. I love, I hate, I cry, I laugh, I make mistakes, I learn, I dream, I hurt, I get hurt . . . I still have not figured out what crime I have committed to endure this kind of wretchedness. I wonder what being human feels like."

For every group that uses media to affirm its humanity, there is another group proclaiming that humanity as irrelevant, or inconvenient, or a lie. One can see this not only in the Middle East conflict, but in movements like Nigeria's "Bring Back Our Girls," which represents victims frequently proclaimed as "forgotten" due to their so-called "nameless and faceless" status. But the girls were never nameless and faceless to the Nigerians who fought, and continue to fight, for their survival. They have names that few learned, faces from which many turned away. The people who refuse to forget are the ones the West has now forgotten.

In all documentation of violence, from memoirs to social media, lies a plea to not forget. There is a reason Netanyahu fears the "telegenically dead." They haunt the world like ghosts—a reminder of what we have done, what we are capable of doing, and the lengths gone to justify it.

Those dehumanized in life become humanized in death. With this realization you mourn not only the dead. You mourn the living too.

—Originally published August 14, 2014

Coda

In Defense of Complaining

n 2006, the Reverend Will Bowen launched a movement called A Complaint Free World. The goal of the movement was to get people to stop expressing "pain, grief, or discontent."

The best way to stop expressing pain, grief, or discontent was to buy Bowen's book and purple bracelets from his website. The bracelets serve as a sartorial censor for those compelled to discuss their problems. Every time you complain, you must switch the bracelet to the other wrist. If you go twenty-one consecutive days without complaining or switching the bracelets, you are rewarded with a Certificate of Happiness.

"Our words indicate our thoughts," the certificate says. "Our thoughts create our world."

In an America built on the reinvention of reality, critical words make people uneasy—and so do those who speak them. In 1996, Alan Greenspan famously chided the financial community for "irrational exuberance." They ignored him, and America became a bubble economy—housing, credit, technology, higher education. Those who warned of collapse were derided and dismissed: they were only complaining.

When the bubbles popped, and the jobs disappeared, and the debt soared, and the desperation hit, Americans were told to stay positive. Stop complaining—things will not be like this forever. Stop complaining—this is the way things have always been. Complainers suffer the cruel imperatives of optimism: lighten up, suck it up, chin up, buck up. In other words: shut up.

The surest way to keep a problem from being solved is to deny that problem exists. Telling people not to complain is a way of keeping social issues from being addressed. It trivializes the grievances of the vulnerable, making the burdened feel like burdens. Telling people not to complain is an act of power, a way of asserting that one's position is more important than another one's pain. People who say "stop complaining" always have the right to stop listening. But those who complain have often been denied the right to speak.

The condemnation of complaining is not unique to America. Dictatorships around the world are famous for self-reported statistics of sky-high happiness. In Uzbekistan, a state run on surveillance, corruption, and torture, 95 percent of the country is said to be content. Last August, one of the openly unhappy 5 percent, a seventy-three-year-old man, filed a complaint about police brutality with neighborhood officials. They arrested him for violating a ban on filing complaints.

The absence of complaining should be taken as a sign that something is rotting in a society. Complaining is beautiful. Complaining should be encouraged. Complaining means you have a chance.

Excuses, Excuses

All social movements are dismissed at some point as complaining. Over time, they are recognized as speaking truth to power.

Last month, I attended the Oslo Freedom Forum, an annual conference that gives the people who challenge repressive regimes a platform to speak. This year's conference featured well-known writers and activists from China, Syria, Bahrain, and other autocratic states. They were there to complain—but it is not thought of as complaining

> The surest way to keep a problem from being solved is to deny that problem exists.

when a prominent advocate speaks about oppression to a crowd. Then it becomes the impartation of knowledge, but no one starts from that. It is a long road from whiner to witness.

Complaint is often perceived as an alternative to action. Those who complain are criticized as "just complaining," instead of "actually doing something." But for marginalized and stigmatized groups—racial and religious minorities, women, the poor, people who lack civic rights—complaining is the first step in removing the shame from a lifetime of being told one's problems are unimportant, nonexistent, or even a cause for gratitude. Complaining alerts the world that the problem is a problem.

In May, President Obama told an audience of African-American graduates at Morehouse, a historically black college in Atlanta, that "there's no longer any room for excuses." He chided young black men for seeing their race as an obstacle, because "whatever hardships you may experience because of your race . . . pale in comparison to the hardships previous generations endured—and overcame."

He told them this in a month when many black public schools were shut down, a black girl was prosecuted for a science project gone awry, rates of black unemployment climbed, and black student loan debt soared. Massive racial inequality was slightly less massive than before, though, so best to ignore structural problems and focus on individual goals.

"No room for excuses" is the cousin of "stop complaining."

It's Always Been Like That!

Another common response to complaining is that the respondent has heard it all before. "That problem has been around forever," this person will say, as if this itself did not attest to the severity of the problem. Long-term complaining indicates that a problem is serious and structural, not that it is hopeless and should continue to be ignored.

Complaints long discounted often grow louder over time. We see this today in the slowly growing movement against labor exploitation in America, a movement that includes everyone from fast food workers to adjunct professors. As the American economy lurches into permanent contingency, everyone is told it is their own fault.

"How can you complain when you didn't get an education?" they tell the striking McDonald's worker. "You thought all that education would get you a job?" they sneer at the striking adjunct.

Complaining creates common ground. In complaints, people find that their problems are not so far apart. Those who dismiss complaints display their own discomfort, the fear that they could be next. When it happens—and it will happen—seek comfort in complaint.

It Could Always Be Worse!

Another common response to complaining is to delegitimize misery by portraying it as a competition. "You're privileged, you have an education," they tell the white-collar unemployed. "You're privileged, you live in America," they tell the poor. "You're privileged, you got out," they tell the exile. "You're privileged, you have food and shelter," they tell the subject of the dictator.

It could always be worse, they say. They don't like to say that it could always be better, because that would require redress.

Ranking complaints is a way to make people feel guilty

for their own struggle, instead of empowered to take action through a collective expression of shared concerns. It stratifies suffering into a hierarchy, creating what writer C. Z. Nnaemeka called an "unexotic underclass" whose problems go ignored. Categorizing the complainers breeds hypocrisy in wealthy nations—where debt-burdened graduates work unpaid internships for NGO's claiming to promote fairness— and the dehumanization of people in poorer countries, who are treated as charity cases without minds of their own.

People hate complaining because they do not like to listen. When you listen to someone complaining, you are forced to acknowledge them as a human being instead of a category. You are forced to witness how social systems are borne out in personal experience, to recognize that hardship hurts, that solutions are not as simple as they seem.

You are forced to trust, and you are forced to care. In complaint lies a path to compassion.

—Originally published June 15, 2013

Epilogue

On January 18, 2017, two days before leaving the White House, Barack Obama addressed America as its president for the last time: "We're going to be okay," he promised citizens anxious not only about Trump's unexpected win, but about the autocratic policies he promised to pass and the extremist cabinet he had assembled.

As you know by now, America was not okay. Our country has had to learn the hard way that laws are only as good as the people who uphold them, that without ethical officials to enforce it, the Constitution is nothing but a piece of paper. Americans have learned that our age-old institutions are weaker than we suspected, that our ability to function as a country rests as much on norms as it does on laws, and that both laws and norms can be shattered.

But Americans have also learned that we are our own

greatest strength. We recognized our rights as we lost them, then we fought for those rights to be returned to us.

The years in which I wrote the essays in this book were marked by the erosion of political and economic stability—an erosion that long preceded the Obama administration, a social crime whose perpetrators were as diverse as its victims. Two wars, a recession, extreme partisanship, and antiquated political structures that could not keep pace with rapid technological change left America vulnerable to autocracy. And autocracy arose in the administration of Donald Trump. Americans have become locked in a constant test of checks and balances, in which a government with authoritarian ambitions fights against a citizenry accustomed to fundamental freedoms: the freedom to assemble, to write, to speak. Freedoms that can no longer be taken for granted.

The Trump administration has created so many new problems that the difficult era of the mid-2010s seem enviable by comparison. Under Trump, we worry anew about nuclear war, violent white supremacists, mass deportation of immigrants, and subterfuge of our most elemental democratic practices—like the right to vote—by hostile foreign parties. We have had to ask new questions, like "To which country does our president's greatest loyalty lie?" We have had to call our representatives every day to beg them not to kill us by revoking access to health care. We have had to live under the whim of a president so fundamentally unstable that we worry one of his stray tweets will lead to war. These problems were previously unfathomable; these are the problems of a country shifting from a flawed democracy into an autocracy.

The motto of dictatorship has long been "It can't happen here," and that willful blindness prompted many pundits to proclaim—during the primary, the election, and after—that Trump would eventually "pivot." But Trump is never going to pivot. His goal has always been to align Americans to his views, to pull the fringes to the center, and to make the extreme mainstream. In many ways, he has succeeded: he has installed white supremacists into positions of power and shifted public expectations of behavior so violently that his ability to give a teleprompter speech without saying something egregiously racist is often lauded as "presidential." These are the delusions of Americans wounded by whiplash, who badly want their country to get back to "normal."

But as understandable as that desire is, it is essential that we remember that "normal" is how we got here. The quieter crises of the pre-Trump era contained their own agonies, ones that have only been exacerbated or that have remained unchanged under his rule. In 2017, our political focus shifted from examining systemic flaws to stopping imminent disasters. But the fundamental problems that preceded Trump's reign have gone unresolved.

Income inequality remains at a level unrivaled in modern U.S. history, as does household debt. Wages remain stagnant or in decline. Higher education remains an exorbitant barrier to middle-class jobs, while middle-class jobs continue to disappear. Geographical inequality, which Trump's team expertly exploited, remains rampant, with prestigious jobs clustered in cities few can afford. The attacks on civil rights that had been gaining steam prior to 2016 have become a state-sanctioned assault on the most vulnerable people: ethnic, racial, or religious minorities; immigrants; LGBT Americans; or others scapegoated on the sidelines in Trump's narrow vision of nationalism.

In the midst of Trump's burgeoning autocracy, a phenomenon that I found jarring has arisen: the region where I live has become central to U.S. political discourse. Suddenly, the coastal politicians and pundits who had scorned the Midwest have become subsumed by it, eagerly seeking every extremist Trump fan they can find, with some media outlets like *The New York Times* interviewing the same people repeatedly. A new caricature has emerged: the righteous Midwestern racist, who is almost always an elderly man from a bottomed-out industrial town whose fealty to Trump is explained solely by his "economic anxiety."

This narrative is as maddening as it is hurtful. It ignores the complexities and diversity of the region while also disregarding serious structural barriers, like new voter ID laws, that so narrowly ensured Trump's victory—a victory that was presented, both by much of the media and by Trump himself, as the revenge of "the forgotten people." But as usual, selective memory has ruled, and many have been forgotten from the category of "the forgotten." Nonwhite Midwesterners vanished from election coverage; ambivalent white Midwestern voters—a category that includes many who voted for Trump—were shunned in favor of faithful fanatics. This misleading narrative is insulting to the groups persecuted by the administration, but it also does the Trump voters themselves no favors, as they too have been hurt by the chaos and callousness of his reign.

The economic anxiety of the Midwest was real, and it continues. But economic anxiety is no excuse for racism or cruelty, and that continues as well. As Trump persecutes his nonwhite targets, media outlets allow the Midwest to stand in as his representative region, which is a convenient way to ignore the prevalence of bigotry in coastal states or among the wealthy and educated. We are still "flyover country," only now all our whites are racists and the rest of our population has disappeared.

My own state, Missouri, has become a model of low-key autocracy, replacing Kansas as the go-to example of American political dysfunction. After Trump's election, the Missouri legislature *lowered* the minimum wage by $2.70, passed a law that made it possible to fire women who use birth control, and handed over private voter data to the Trump administration even as other conservative states resisted. Missouri even became the first state to receive a travel warning from the NAACP declaring it was too dangerous for black people to visit. The nightmare scenarios that some envisioned for the United States as Trump consolidated power play out in Missouri every day, along with the widespread economic devastation and social unrest that preceded his election and remained unresolved.

But resistance remains as well. The biggest barrier to a strong resistance is a refusal to acknowledge not only that the worst can happen, but that it has happened before.

"Who could have predicted a Trump win?" pundits pondered, and the answer was often blacks, Latinos, Muslims, and residents of the ignored heartland regions where he gained popularity—the people whom Trump treated as target practice, and people in regions he targeted for votes. These folks are the "no one" in the oft-said and inaccurate phrase of "no one saw it coming," a phrase that indicts the fool that utters it. *Many* Americans saw it coming, but their warnings were often dismissed as implausible or, worse, hysterical, when they were simply logical predictions based on lived experience. The people pushed to the margins in the heartland knew it would not be okay, because it had never been okay. For many, the hypotheticals had already happened.

Trump's win was fairly easy to predict; how the public would react was far less certain. But from the moment his administration took power, Americans have been fighting back against their president's autocratic aims. They have been fighting for themselves, and they have been fighting for people they don't know. As social trust has eroded, they fight to rebuild it, not through blind faith in a failing system, but by exhibiting the willingness to stand up for each other and for constitutional principles that were not being honored in practice. What has become known as "the resistance" is simply people helping each other, an idea that is subversive under an administration that peddles cruelty as conventional. Some speculated that the resistance would burn out, but people do not burn out when they are fighting to survive.

With nearly every day bringing a crisis that would have seemed unimaginable a decade before, America's famous optimism has begun to fade. This may seem like a loss, but it is a gift, because the denial of encroaching darkness was what prevented so many from seeing the light. The insistence that "things would work themselves out" circumvented compassion, it negated solutions, and it made people enraged when their expectations were not met. Assurances that their anxiety was unfounded left people ashamed to speak out. Far fewer people are afraid to speak out now.

Repairing the damage that has been done to American society will take a long time. Underneath the explosive residue of the Trump administration lies the rot of systemic problems that have lingered for decades. They will not be fixed overnight. But they will never be fixed if they are not addressed with honesty, pragmatism, and compassion. The willingness of so many Americans to do that today gives me hope, however tentative, that the conditions described in this book may someday seem unfamiliar, that they will become the relics of an era remembered best as a cautionary tale.

—September 2017

Acknowledgments

The print version of this book is six years in the making, and they have been a very memorable, exciting, and painful six years. If I were to list all the people to whom I'm grateful, you'd have another book, so apologies in advance to those who I omit.

First I'd like to thank my editor at Al Jazeera English, Naz Khan, who took a chance on me when I was a PhD student, let me speak my mind unimpeded on controversial topics, and was a great source of support over our years working together. Similar thanks to my literary agent, Robert Lecker, who sought me out before my work achieved mass popularity, and proved a steadfast advisor throughout this process. Thanks also to the team at Macmillan, including: Whitney Frick, the former executive editor at Macmillan who first introduced this project to Flatiron Books; Bryn Clark, the associate editor who brought the print version to fruition; my Flatiron publicist, Amelia Possanza; and the rest of the production team at Macmillan.

Thanks to everyone who has worked as my editor in the years after I left Al Jazeera, especially Amberly McTeer at *The Globe and Mail*; Meredith Bennet-Smith at *Quartz* and NBC News; Anjali Khosla at Fast Company; and Erica Moore at *De Correspondent*. You all helped make me a stronger writer. Thanks also to Joy-Ann Reid at MSNBC for giving me a platform to discuss the Trump regime and other social ills on television.

You may notice that I am largely thanking women in this section. To a large degree, it has been women who supported my writing and who did not dismiss my concerns about our country's future as hyperbole or hysteria. We need more women in editorial positions and more female writers covering issues like politics, technology, and the economy. We need more women in positions of power in general. I hope I will have many more women to thank in the years to come.

Like most people, I have a love/hate relationship with Twitter, but I am very grateful for the friends I have made there over the years. I'm particularly grateful to Linda Tirado, Leah McElrath, Sydette Harry, Andrea Chalupa, Imani Gandy, Melissa McEwan, and Mikki Kendall for half a decade of feedback, support, and survival tips. I'd also like to thank my friends in St. Louis, particularly those involved in the Ferguson protest movement who stayed in the region and continue to work for change against long odds, and especially my friend and occasional cowriter Umar Lee.

My deepest thanks to my readership, who have stuck

with me through tumultuous times. I'm very lucky to have an audience as engaged and informative as you, and I appreciate all the emails, letters, and tweets over the years. I hope you are as pleased with this updated version as I am.

Most of all, I'd like to thank my family. In memoriam: thank you Emily and Leo Kendzior and Hope and Sherman Tonkonow for your love, advice, and making me the person I am; I miss you. Thanks also to my parents, Barbara and Larry; my in-laws Sally, Phil, Liz, and Dave; my sister, Lizzie, and her husband, Mike; and my nieces and nephews Jack, Kate, Karl, and Julia. A huge debt of gratitude for my extremely patient husband, Pete, who has put up with me throughout this wild ride.

But above all, thanks go to my two favorite people, Emily and Alex. I wrote *The View from Flyover Country* with the aim of exposing problems we all face and contributing to a better world for you and your generation. Hopefully by the time you're old enough to read my work, it will seem as far-fetched as fiction. I love you.